SHADE
OF
HIS HAND

Discovery House Publishers

Books, music, and videos that feed the soul with the Word of God

Box 3566 Grand Rapids, MI 49501

SHADE
OF
HIS HAND

OSWALD CHAMBERS

*Published through special arrangement with the
Oswald Chambers Publications Association Ltd.*

CONTENTS

Publisher's Foreword

These lectures on Ecclesiastes were the last messages spoken by Oswald Chambers to the British troops in Egypt during World War I. He died on November 15, 1917. How appropriate that his final words dealt with the truth of a book of the Bible frequently ignored by Bible students, the book of Ecclesiastes.

The writer challenges modern men and women to learn early in life the vital truth that pleasure, in its purist form, and the meaning of life must be found in God, and God alone. Otherwise, life will be seen as disaster, ineffable sadness and tragedy.

Oswald Chambers consistently reminds his audience that God, in redemption, reverses the natural order of chaos and destruction. He brings meaning and purpose and deepest joy to life. The only way we can find relief and the right interpretation of things as they are is by basing our faith and confidence in God, and by remembering that man's chief end is to glorify God and enjoy Him forever.

This is Chambers' legacy. Discovery House Publishers is proud to issue it in a new edition for a new generation of readers.

The Publisher

Foreword to Previous Edition

These talks on Ecclesiastes were given by my friend Oswald Chambers at the Y.M.C.A. Hut, Zeitoun, Egypt, to British Troops in October 1917. They are a verbatim report of what really were the last lectures he ever delivered, for he was called from the midst of his happy, arduous, fruitful toil among the soldiers into the immediate presence of his Lord on November 15, 1917.

These last expository talks ought to be taken in the light of his former teaching. Those who know his other books will profit most by this one. In the earlier books he shows the process of salvation as it works out in the inner life of a man. Here we see it in its relation to the everyday world outside us.

Does Ecclesiastes teach that life is not worth living? That gloomy tale would not be worth telling. Oswald Chambers interprets its message as being—Life is not worth living apart from redemption. This is a book of wisdom for today. It shows how it is possible for a redeemed man to glorify God amid all the interplay of life's forces, in work and play, in study, in recreation, in home life or social intercourse. Life apart from redeeming Love is full of sin and sorrow, guile and cruelty, callous selfishness and numbing despair. This book takes full account of all that. It anticipates many of the problems facing the young life of today and brings to their solution the one and only key, the realization of the Lord Jesus in every relationship of life.

David Lambert

Additional Note

Oswald Chambers died before he could finish this exposition of Ecclesiastes. However, to make the book complete, I have added notes on both the first and final chapters.

May this volume of penetrating and perceptive reality meet a vital need in these days of disillusionment and despair in so many quarters of our modern civilization.

Arthur Neil
Editor, O.C.P.A.
December 1990

Rationalism Hard Pressed
Ecclesiastes 1

"Myself when young did eagerly frequent
Doctor and Saint, and heard great Argument
About it and about, but evermore
Came out by the same Door wherein I went.

With them the Seed of Wisdom did I sow,
And with mine own hand wrought to make it grow,
And this was all the Harvest that I reaped,
I came like Water and like Wind I go."

—Omar Khayyam

It is important to notice the difference between the wisdom of the Hebrews and the wisdom of the Greeks. The wisdom of the Hebrews is based on an accepted belief in God; that is, it does not try to find out whether or not God exists, all its beliefs are based on God, and in the actual whirl of things as they are, all its mental energy is bent on practical living. The wisdom of the Greeks, which is the wisdom of our day, is speculative; that is, it is concerned with the origin of things, with the riddle of the universe. Consequently, the best of our writers is not given to practical living (see 1 Ki. 4:29-32).

The book of Job was produced by Solomon and his school of wisdom, and in it we see worked out, according to Hebrew wisdom, how a man may suffer in the actual condition of things. The sufferings of Job were not in order to perfect him (see Job 1:8). The explanation of Job's sufferings was that God and Satan had made a battleground of his soul, and the honor of God was at stake.

The sneer of Satan was that no one loved God for His own sake but only for what God gave him. Satan was allowed to destroy all his blessings and yet Job did not curse God; he clung to it that the great desire of his heart was God Himself and not His blessings. Job lost everything he possessed, including his creed; the one thing he did not lose was his hold on God, "Though He slay me, yet will I trust Him."

The value of the book of Job is not in what it teaches, but that it expresses suffering, and the inscrutability of suffering.

In the book of Psalms, wisdom is applied to things as they are and to prayer. The book of Proverbs applies wisdom to the practical relationships of life, and Ecclesiastes applies wisdom to the enjoyment of things as they actually are; there is no phase of life missed out, and it is shown that enjoyment is only possible by being related to God.

The record of the whirl of things as they are is marvelously stated in these books of wisdom: Job—how to suffer; Psalms—how to pray; Proverbs—how to act; Ecclesiastes—how to enjoy; Song of Solomon—how to love.

The Wisdom of the Hebrews
Proverbs 8:22-36

The wisdom of the Hebrews does not set out to discover whether God is, nor does it enter into speculating enquiries as to the origin of sin. Belief in God is never questioned, and on that basis Hebrew wisdom sets out to deal with practical things as they are.

The basis of things is not rational, but tragic. Reason is our guide among facts as they are, but reason cannot account for things being as they are. This does not mean that a man is not to use his reason; reason is the biggest gift he has. The rationalist says that everything in between birth and death is discernible by human reason; but the actual experience of life is that things do not run in a reasonable way, there are irrational elements to be reckoned with.

The Old Testament is coming to its own just now; we have been too patronizing. We always get out of touch with the Bible attitude to things when we come to it with our own conclusions. For instance, the Bible does not prove the existence of God, nor does it prove that Jesus Christ is the Son of God. The Bible was written to confirm the faith of those who already believe in God. We are apt to come to the conclusion that the Bible is tepid. Why, some of the most heroic and drastic thinking is within the covers of the Bible! St. John and St. Paul reconstructed religious thought, quoting from no one; there are no thinkers like them, yet it has been fashionable to belittle them.

The Wisdom of the Greeks
1 Corinthians 1:19-25

Our modern wisdom, which is the wisdom of the Greeks, is three times removed from actual facts. It is mental; we are busy trying to find out the origin of things. It is a type of wisdom that does not find its home in the Bible. The intellectual order of life does not take things as it finds them, it makes us shut our eyes to actual facts and try to live only in the ideal world. The wisdom of the Greeks tells us how things should be—there ought to be no sin, no war, no devil, no sickness, no injustice; but these things are! It is no use to turn ourselves into ostriches mentally and ignore them. Solomon is fearless in facing facts as they are. No room is allowed either in the Old or New Testament for mysticism pure and simple, because that will mean sooner or later an aloofness from actual life, a kind of contempt expressed or implied by a superior attitude, by occult relationships and finer sensibilities. That attitude is never countenanced in the Bible. The Mount of Transfiguration may serve for a symbol of mysticism—"Peter answered and said to Jesus, 'Lord, it is good for us to be here; . . . let us make here three tabernacles.'" But there quickly followed the transition to the demon-possessed valley. The test of mountain-top experiences, of mysticism, of visions of God and of solitarinesses is when you are "in the soup" of actual circumstances. It is not a question of living a blind life in the brain away from actuality, not of living in dawns or on mountaintops; but of bringing what you see there straight down to the valley where things are sordid, and living out the vision there.

Practical Experiment
Ecclesiastes 1:1-11

In the book of Ecclesiastes we deal with the actual condition of the things we are in, which is the arena for manifesting the hold we have on God in the unseen.

Constant Obliteration of Conscious Effort
" 'Vanity of Vanities,' says the Preacher; 'vanity of vanities; all is vanity.' What profit has a man from all his labor in which he toils under the sun? One generation passes away, and another generation comes; but the earth abides forever" (vv. 2-4).

"Vanity," that is, ephemeral, not conceit, but fleeting, here and gone as a day. Everything man has ever done is constantly being obliterated; everything a man fights for and lives for passes; he has so many years to live and then it is finished. This is neither fiction nor dumps. In true thinking of things as they are, there is always a bedrock of unmitigated sadness. Optimism is either religious or temperamental. No man who thinks and faces life as it actually is, can be other than pessimistic. There is no way out unless he finds it by religious faith or is blinded by his temperament. The summing up of all practical life is that the basis of things is tragic. Sum up your life as it actually is, and, unless you look at actual things from a religious or a temperamental or an intellectual standpoint, everything is to be said for this philosophy: Eat, drink, and be merry, for tomorrow we die. If rationalism is the basis of things, that is undoubtedly the most reasonable thing to do. But if the basis of things is tragic, then the Bible standpoint comes nearer the solution, and Nietzsche is nearer the truth than any rationalist. Nietzsche declares that the basis of things is tragic, and that the way out is by the merciless superman; the Bible reveals that the basis of things is tragic, and that the way out is by redemption. We say that man is in process of evolution—a magnificent promise of what he is going to be! The wisdom of the Hebrews looks at man's history and attainments and says—What a magnificent ruin of what he was created to be!

Very few of us think unblinded by a religious or a temperamental point of view; we are not capable of it. We are blinded either by religion, or temperament, or by thickheadedness. To look at things as they are, with the superb wisdom and understanding and disillusioned eye of Solomon, takes a Solomon to do it. Another man did it with the knowledge and understanding of Solomon, and he was Ibsen.

He saw facts as they are clearly, without losing his head, and without any faith in God he summed it all up—no forgiveness, no escape from penalty or retribution, it is absolutely and inexorably certain that the end of things is disaster. In Shakespeare's writings there is an undercurrent of faith which makes him the peculiarly valuable writer he is, and makes him more at home to those who understand the Bible point of view than to those who do not.

Continual Oblivion of Cosmic Effects

"The sun also rises, and the sun goes down, and hastens to the place where it arose. The wind goes toward the south, and turns around to the north; the wind whirls about continually, and comes again on its circuit" (vv. 5-6).

Everything that happens in nature is continually being obliterated and beginning again. What Solomon says is not merely a poetical statement. A sunset or a sunrise may thrill you for a half a minute, so may beautiful music or a song, but the sudden aftermath is a terrific, and almost eternal sadness. Lovers always think of what one would do if the other died; it is more than drivel. Immediately you strike the elemental in war or in nature or in love, you come to the basis of ineffable sadness and tragedy. You feel that things ought to be full of joy and brightness, but they are not. You will never find the abiding order of joy in the haphazard, and yet the meaning of Christianity is that God's order comes to a man in the haphazard.

There is a difference between God's will and God's order. Take the case of two boys born in the slums. One determines to get out of it, and carves out for himself an honorable career; he gets at God's order in the middle of His permissive will. The other sinks down in despair and remains where he is. God's order is—no sin, no sickness, no devil, no war; His permissive will is things as they are.

Common Origin of Changing Experiences

"All the rivers run into the sea, yet the sea is not full; to the place from which the rivers come, there they return again. All things are full of labor; man cannot express it. The eye is not satisfied with seeing, nor the ear filled with hearing. That which has been is what will be, that which is done is what will be done, and there is nothing new under the sun" (vv. 7-9).

You may try to rest in any phase of actual existence, says Solomon, but apart from your relationship to God, you are better dead. Unless you bank your faith in God, you will not only be wrongly related in practical life and have your heart broken, but you will break other things you touch (see Matt. 18:6-7).

Counterfeit Originality of Casual Expressions

"Is there anything of which it may be said, 'See, this is new'? It has already been in ancient times before us. There is no remembrance of former things, nor will there be any remembrance of things that are to come by those who will come after" (vv. 10-11).

It is only when we are ignorant that we believe in originality. We have such magnificent "forgetteries" that we obliterate the whole of human history for the discovery we have made, and say—This is original. Solomon says the whole thing is an incessant and appalling weariness.

Personal Experience
Ecclesiastes 1:12-13

The Bible indicates that a man always fails on his strongest point. Abraham, the man of faith, fell through unbelief; Moses, the meek man, fell through losing his temper; Elijah, the courageous man, fell through losing heart; and

Solomon, the most colossally wise, wealthy, luxurious, superb king, fell through grovelling, sensual idolatry.

Actual Condition of Thought

"I, the Preacher, was king over Israel in Jerusalem. And I set my heart to seek and search out by wisdom concerning all that is done under heaven; this grievous task God has given to the sons of man, by which they may be exercised" (vv.12-13).

These are the words of a man who has tried and experienced the things he speaks of. We say there ought not to be war, there ought to be no devil, no suffering, and we fuss and fume; but these things *are!* If we lived in the clouds, it would be different; but we are here. "If only I was not where I am!" It is in the present dilemma that practical wisdom is required.

I believe that the apparent atheism of Job and of men today is more wholesome than to believe in a God about whom you have to tell lies to prove He is God. Voltaire tiraded against the God who was masqueraded before men in his day. In a mental stress of weather it is better not to believe in a Being who has not the clear sense of justice we have, than to believe in One who is an outrage to our sense of justice; better to "snatch at the damnation" of such a Being than to accept His salvation.

We are driven back every time to Jesus Christ—"I am the Way, the Truth, and the Life." Have I seen Him, or do I see only that which echoes myself? Am I prepared to see in Jesus Christ the outlines of the true character of God, which is holiness? We *perceive* our friend while we only *see* the other man, and it is the same with the perception of God (John 3:3).

Jesus Christ is God-Man. God in essence cannot come anywhere near us. Almighty God does not matter to me, He is in the clouds. To be of any use to me, He must come down to the domain in which I live; and I do not live in the clouds but on the earth. The doctrine of the Incarnation is that God did come down into our domain. The wisdom of God, the Word of God, the exact expression of God, was manifest in the flesh. That is the great doctrine of the New Testament—dust and Deity made one. The pure gold of Deity is of no use to us unless it is amalgamated in the right alloy, the pure divine working on the basis of the pure human: God and humanity one, as in our Lord Jesus Christ. There is only one God to the Christian, and His name is Jesus Christ, and in Him we see mirrored what the human race will be like on the basis of redemption—a perfect one-ness between God and man. Jesus Christ has the power of reproducing Himself by regeneration, the power of introduc-ing into us His own heredity, so that dust and Deity again become one.

Absolute Conundrum of Thinking
"I have seen all the works that are done under the sun; and indeed, all is vanity and grasping for the wind. What is crooked cannot be made straight, and what is lacking cannot be numbered" (vv. 14-15).

Here we note the observation of comprehensive futili-ty in man's activities. There is no meaning to it. Yet, there is implanted in man the insistent instinct and impe-tus for order and system. In his reasoning he recognizes the ideal for harmonious issues in what he does and why he does it. But it all goes "hay-wire" and it only con-tributes to his dilemma and despair. There are vital fac-tors absent to resolve the puzzle of his existence and actions. The enigma of foiled purpose with its perverted outcome is due to the twist in his fundamental disposition which disorientates him at the core of his being. There is only one who can make the crooked places straight and the rough places smooth, and He is the Lord Jesus Christ who is both the wisdom and the power of God to effect both inner righteousness of character and outward righteousness of conduct.

Applied Cultures of Time

"I communed with my heart, saying, 'Look, I have attained greatness, and have gained more wisdom than all who were before me in Jerusalem. My heart has understood great wisdom and knowledge' " (vv. 16-17)

Solomon was no dullard. His diligence was unsurpassed to acquire all he could with everything necessary at his disposal. He was a master in philosophy and cultural pursuits in order to enhance mankind for the best. Every avenue was explored to achieve the greatest benefits possible for humanity's welfare. But he discovered that reality was both elusive and exasperating.

However wise the idea and ideal, the world's philosophy brings about the cultural shock that man's best proposed and ordered schemes go sadly and tragically astray. The very noblest effort of human ingenuity brings us to the conclusive verdict that we don't have the key to reality and that ultimately we know nothing. The mystery of life is really and regretfully the misery of life. Why? Because the basis of things is tragic and no logic can alter this drastic fact that is rooted in man's corrupt nature. It is just here where the redemption wrought by Jesus Christ is to be known in all its transforming ministry to break the vicious entail of sin and give newness of life and a glorious hope, according to the good pleasure of God's will and the riches of His grace.

Ascertained Cruelty of Truth

"And I set my heart to know wisdom and to know madness and folly. I perceived that this also is grasping for the wind. For in much wisdom is much grief, and he who increases knowledge increases sorrow" (v. 18).

Solomon sums up the matter as follows: If you try to find enjoyment in the order of things, you will end in vexation and disaster. If you try to find enjoyment in knowledge, you only increase your capacity for sorrow and agony and distress. The only way you can find relief and the right interpretation of things as they are is by basing your faith in God, and by remembering that man's chief end is to glorify God and enjoy Him forever. Jesus Christ is the one who can transmute everything we come across.

In the Thick of It
Ecclesiastes 2

But whoso wants God only and lets life go,
Seeks Him with sorrow and pursues Him far,
And finds Him weeping, and in no long time
Agaïn the High and Unapproachable
Evanishing escapeth, and that man
Forgets the life and struggle of the soul,
Falls from his hope and dreams it was a dream,
Yet back again perforce with sorrow and shame
Who once hath known Him must return, not long
Can cease from loving, nor endures alone
The dreadful interspace of dreams and day,
Once quick with God, nor is content as those
Who look into each other's eyes and seek
To find out strong enough to uphold the earth,
Or sweet enough to make it heaven; aha,
Whom seek they or whom find? For in all the world
There is none but Thee, my God, there is none but Thee."
—Myers

If a man faces actual things as they are and thinks them right
out, he must be a pessimist. Most of us are either too thick-

headed, or too prejudiced, or too religious, to think right out to the bottom board of things, until the tension comes and obliges us to face them; then we find out who are the men who point the finest way of thinking.

The Culture of Revolt
Ecclesiastes 2:1-11

Revolt in Every Passion
"I said in my heart, 'Come now, I will test you with mirth; therefore enjoy pleasure'; but surely, this also was vanity. I said of laughter, 'It is madness'; and of mirth, 'What does it accomplish?' " (vv. 1-2).

In this chapter Solomon gives himself up to the philosophical line—Why should a man not take life as he finds it? Solomon was sick of trying to find any rationality at the back of things, he revolted from it, and indulged every passion and appetite without restraint. Always distinguish between the man who is naturally given to passion and appetite and the man who goes into these things from revolt. There is an irony and a bitterness and a criminality about the man who does it in revolt. In the same way there is a difference between laughter that is natural and laughter that is a revolt. The man who discovers that he can find no way out may go into the pigsty and let every passion have its way; but when he has been gripped by purity and has seen God if only for one minute, he may try and live in a pigsty but he will find he cannot, there is something that produces misery and longing even while he lets loose his passions.

Restraint in Epicurean Appetite
"I searched in my heart how to gratify my flesh with wine,

while guiding my heart with wisdom, and how to lay hold on folly, till I might see what was good for the sons of men to do under heaven all the days of their lives" (v. 3).

Solomon based all his knowledge of art and education on the desire to satisfy with restraint and wisdom all the natural life of a man. If the basis of life is rational, that should be sufficient. Epicurus was a philosopher of the first order, and he tried to make the basis of life a judicious handling of the pleasures of life, especially the pleasures of the table. "I searched in my heart how to gratify my flesh with wine, while guiding my heart with wisdom," not living the life of a beast, but trying to find out whether it was possible by judiciously handling the right appetites of life to find satisfaction, but that too was vanity. This was not an experiment a man might think of trying, but an experiment that was tried, and tried by a man who had opportunities such as no one before or since has had of proving it.

Reconstruction in Astheticism
"I made my works great, I built myself houses, and planted myself vineyards. I made myself gardens and orchards, and I planted all kinds of fruit trees in them. I made myself water-pools from which to water the growing trees of the grove. I acquired male and female servants, and had servants born in my house. Yes, I had greater possessions of herds and flocks than all who were in Jerusalem before me. I also gathered for myself silver and gold and the special treasures of kings and of the provinces. I acquired male and female singers, the delights of the sons of men, and musical instruments of all kinds. So I became great and excelled more than all who were before me in Jerusalem. Also my wisdom remained with me. Whatever my eyes desired I did not keep from

them. I did not withhold my heart from any pleasure, for my heart rejoiced in all my labor; and this was my reward from all my labor" (vv. 4-10).

Solomon indicates in these verses that he reconstructed his life on the aesthetic basis to try and find joy there. On the aesthetic line a man is apt to think he is of a different order from the generality of men, and that whatever pleases his senses is legitimate for him to have. "Whatever my eyes desired I did not keep from them." But we have to remember that the first civilization was founded by a murderer on murder, and that all aesthetic developments are based on that level. The origin of art and poetry and music was with God, but their development has been on a wrong basis, and consequently they have been prostituted away from their true service in a man's life. Aestheticism is all very well for the kingdom of heaven, but it won't do for the kingdom of earth. This is an anti-modern view.

Reaction in Each Affinity

"Then I looked on all the works that my hands had done and on the labor in which I had toiled; and indeed all was vanity and grasping for the wind. There was no profit under the sun" (v. 11).

This is deep, profound pessimism. All the books of Wisdom in the Bible prove that the only result of sheer thinking on the basis of rationalism is pessimism, fathomlessly profound. The reason most of us are not pessimistic is either that we are religious or we have a temperament that is optimistic. The basis of life is tragic, and the only way out is by a personal relationship to God on the ground of redemption. Solomon deliberately revolted against everything and found there was no satisfaction in anything he tried.

The Culture of Restraint
Ecclesiastes 2:12-23

Nature of Right Estimation

"Then I turned myself to consider wisdom and madness and folly; for what can the man do who succeeds the king?—Only what he has already done. Then I saw that wisdom excels folly as light excels darkness. The wise man's eyes are in his head, but the fool walks in darkness. Yet I myself perceived that the same event happens to them all" (vv. 12-14).

If a man chooses a right path, does that mean he will find joy? No. Job, for instance, found it did not. He believed that God would bless and prosper the man who trusted in Him, but Job's beliefs were flatly contradicted by his actual experience. Solomon says he tried folly, but found it stupid; a man is an idiot to live like a beast; the best thing to do is to make a right estimate of things.

Nemesis of Reasonable Excellence

"So I said in my heart, 'As it happens to the fool, it also happens to me, and why was I then more wise?' Then I said in my heart, 'This also is vanity.' For there is no more remembrance of the wise than of the fool forever, since all that now is will be forgotten in the days to come, and how does a wise man die? As the fool! Therefore I hated life because the work that was done under the sun was grievous to me, for all is vanity and grasping for the wind. Then I hated all my labor in which I had toiled under the sun, because I must leave it to the man who will come after me. And who knows whether he will be a wise man or a fool? Yet he will rule over all my labor in which I toiled and in which I have shown myself wise under the sun. This also is vanity" (vv. 15-19).

You may do the right thing, says Solomon, but it will end in disaster; reasonable excellence has the same nemesis as revolt. It is no use trying to find true joy in being either a fool or a wise man. Solomon drives us back every time to the one thing, that a man's chief end is to glorify God and enjoy Him forever. Today there is a revolt against the wisdom of the Hebrews and the wisdom expressed in the New Testament. We don't *think* on the Bible lines, consequently we talk the most ridiculous platitudes. It is absurd to be an ostrich. Solomon would not allow himself to be one, neither will the man who sees life fair and square as it is today.

The only way we can enjoy our "tree of life" is by fulfilling the purpose of our creation. Jesus Christ prayed "that they may have My joy fulfilled in themselves." The thing that kept Jesus Christ all through was not that He held aloof from actual things, but that He had a kingdom within. He did not hold aloof when men saw Him and they said, "Look, a glutton and a winebibber, a friend of tax collectors and sinners!" Our Lord's whole life was rooted and grounded in God, consequently He was never wearied or cynical.

"Nihilism" of Revolving Experience
"Therefore I turned my heart and despaired of all the labor in which I had toiled under the sun. For there is a man whose labor is with wisdom, knowledge, and skill; yet he must leave his heritage to a man who has not labored for it. This also is vanity and a great evil. For what has man for all his labor, and for the striving of his heart with which he has toiled under the sun? For all his days are sorrowful, and his work grievous; even in the night his heart takes no rest. This also is vanity" (vv. 20-23).

Everything ends the same way, though I have been good and clean and respectable, my end will be the same as the brute. Though I labor all my days, I shall end the same way as the man who has not labored. These are not wild statements, they are the statements of a man who knew what he was talking about. If Solomon is blind to the issues of life, then the teaching of Christianity is unmitigated nonsense. Some folks are persuaded that it is; they are still cocksure, and have the notion that the kingdom of God can be brought in without the Redemption—all that is needed is to put certain wise restrictions in vogue. Solomon says he tried to do that, but it all ended the same as if he had lived like a fool.

Emerging out of it all comes one voice—"I am the Way, the Truth, and the Life." The way out is not by intellect nor by aesthetics, but through conscience in contact with Christ.

The Culture of Religion

To serve God in order to gain heaven, is not the teaching of Christianity. Satisfaction cannot be found in gain, but only in a personal relationship to God. The presentation made by a false evangelism is that Jesus Christ taught a person must have his own soul saved, be delivered from hell and get a pass for heaven, and when one is taken and the other left, he must look out that he is the one taken. Could anything be more diametrically opposed to what Jesus Christ did teach, or more unlike the revelation of God given in the Bible? A man is not to serve God for the sake of gain, but to get to the place when the whole of his life is seen as a personal relationship to God.

"The Cult of the Passing Moment"
"There is nothing better for a man than that he should eat

and drink, and that his soul should enjoy good in his labor. This also, I saw, was from the hand of God" (v. 24).

One great essential lesson in Christianity is that God's order comes to us in the haphazard. We are men and women, we have appetites, we have to live on this earth, and things do happen by chance; what is the use of saying they do not? "One of the most immutable things on earth is mutability." Your life and mine is a bundle of chance. It is absurd to say it is foreordained for you to have so many buttons on your shirt and if that is not foreordained, then nothing is. If things were foreordained there would be no sense of responsibility at all. A false spirituality makes us look to God to perform a miracle instead of doing our duty. We have to see that when we do our duty in faith in God. Jesus Christ undertakes to do everything a man cannot do, but not what a man can do. Things do happen by chance, and if we know God, we recognize that His order comes to us in that way. We live in this haphazard order of things, and we have to maintain the abiding order of God in it. The doctrine of the sacrament teaches the conveying of God's presence to us through the common elements of bread and wine. We are not to seek success or prosperity. If we can get hold of our relationship to God in eating and drinking, we are on the right basis of things.

The Conception of the Prevailing Master
"For who can eat, or who can have enjoyment more than I?" (v. 25).

The way I eat and drink will show who I regard as my master. Do I regard the restraining wisdom in me as master, or do I regard God as Master? The note of false Christianity is abstinence from marriage and from meats—Live away up on the mount; that is, do what no human being can do. If a man cannot prove his religion in the valley, it is not worth anything. Beware of a religion which makes you neglect the basis of your ordinary life. If you can be a beast, you can also be a son of God. "The Son of Man came eating and drinking .... Have you any food here? .... And He took it and ate in their presence." When once a man has learned to get at God's order in the passing minute and to know that his prevailing Master is God, then he is on the right track. Every other basis ends in disaster.

The Center of Providential Mystery

"For God gives wisdom and knowledge and joy to a man who is good in His sight; but to the sinner He gives the work of gathering and collecting, that he may give to him who is good before God. This also is vanity and grasping for the wind" (v. 26).

There is a difference between God's order and God's permissive will. We say that God will see us through if we trust Him—"I prayed for my boy, and he was spared in answer to my prayer." Does that mean that the man who was killed was not prayed for, or that prayers for him were not answered? It is wrong to say that in the one case the man was delivered by prayer but not in the other. It is a misunderstanding of what Jesus Christ reveals. Prayer alters a man on the inside, alters his mind and his attitude to things. The point of praying is not that we get things from God, but that we learn by prayer to detect the difference between God's order and God's permissive will. God's order is—no pain, no sickness, no devil, no war, no sin: His permissive will is all these things, the "soup" we are in just now. What a man needs to do is to get hold of God's order in the kingdom on the inside, and then he will begin to see how to handle the riddle of the universe on the outside.

The problem of the man who deals with practical things is not the problem of the universe, but the problem within his own breast. When I can see where the beast in me will end and where the wise man in me will end; when I have discovered that the only thing that will last is a personal relationship to God, then it will be time for me to solve the problems around me. When once a man begins to know "the plague of his own heart," it knocks the metaphysics out of him. It is in the actual circumstances of my life that I have to find out whether the wisdom of worshiping God can steer me. Solomon says nothing else can.

In the Whirl
Ecclesiastes 3:1-15

"He fixed thee midst this dance
Of plastic circumstance,
This present thou forsooth would'st fain arrest,
Machinery just meant
To give thy soul its bent,
Try thee and turn thee forth, sufficiently impressed.

Then, welcome each rebuff
That turns earth's smoothness rough,
Each sting that bids nor sit nor stand but go!
Be our joys three parts pain!
Strive and hold cheap the strain,
Learn, nor account the pang, dare, never grudge the
throe."

—Robert Browning

When we are hurt, we are apt to become cynical; cynicism is a sign that the hurt is recent. A mature mind is never cynical. Solomon is not speaking cynically; he goes right down to the facts of life, and comes to the conclusion that there is no way out. There is no way out through reason or intellect; the only way out is on the Bible line, redemption.

Robert Browning wrote from the standpoint of Hebrew wisdom, that of unshakable confidence in God, but he also wrote with the mind of Solomon or Ibsen or Shakespeare for the actual facts of life. He blinks at nothing, yet underneath is the confidence that the basis of a right direction of things is not a man's reason but his strong faith that God is not unjust; and that the man who hangs on to the honor of God will come out all right.

Dispensational Durations
Ecclesiastes 3:1

"To everything there is a season, a time for every purpose under heaven."

The dispensations of God are discernable only to the Spirit of God. If we mistake the dispensations of God to mean something we can see, we are off the track. Solomon is strong on the fact that God has made certain unalterable durations, but he does not say, as St. Augustine and Calvin did, that therefore God is tied up by His own laws. There is a most penetrating criticism of Carlyle by Barry—he said that Carlyle was the intellectual logical result of hyper-Calvinism.

Whenever we put theology or a plan of salvation or any line of explanation before a man's personal relationship to God, we depart from the Bible line, because religion in the Bible is not faith in the rule of God, but faith in the God who rules. If we put our faith in a credal exposition of God and our creed goes to the winds, as, for instance, Job's creed went, our faith will go too. The only thing to do is to "hang on" in confidence in God. "Then will I go . . . unto God, my exceeding joy." Our joy in God depends on what happens. The thing that really sustains is not that we feel happy in God, but that God's joy is our energy, and that when we get out of this "shell" we shall find an explanation that will justify our faith in Him.

There are certain dispensational things for which God is responsible, birth and death. Inside the limits of birth and death people have liberty to produce what they like. We base all our thinking and reasoning on space and time, hence our difficulty when we think about God or the hereafter. We think at once of limits that will not hold after this order of things. There is no space or time with Almighty God. We cannot think beyond the limits of birth and death; if we are to know anything beyond them, it must be by revelation.

Before a man can make us understand the symbols he uses, he must take ideas we already have in our minds and put them into new combinations. It is only when we receive a like apocalyptic spirit of St. John or Ezekiel that we can understand what they are talking about. Jesus Christ did not use figurative language in talking about the hereafter. He said, "Do not let your heart be troubled" and "My business is with the hereafter." Our business is to live a godly life in the present order of things, and not to push out beyond the durations God has placed as limits.

Within the limits of birth and death I can do as I like; but I cannot make myself unborn, neither can I escape death, those two limits are there. I have nothing to do with placing the limits, but within them I can produce what my disposition chooses. Whether I have a distressful time or a joyful time depends on what I do in between the limits of the durations.

"For by Him all things were created" (see Col. 1:16). Did Jesus Christ then create sin? Sin is not a creation, sin is a relationship set up in time between the creation called man and the being who became the devil, whereby man took the rule over himself. My claim to my right to myself—that is the disposition of sin. The Bible reveals that God holds people responsible for acts of sin they commit, but not for the disposition of sin that they have inherited. (See Rom. 5:12.) God Himself has deliberately accepted the responsibility for sin, and the proof that He has done so is the cross of Jesus Christ.

In dealing with practical life we find the fundament of tragedy underlying everything. Fatalism means I am the sport of a force about which I know nothing; faith is trust in a God whose ways I do not know, but whose character I do know. The Bible point of view is that God is ruling and reigning, and that His character is holy. "Though He slay me, yet will I trust Him"—that is the final heroism of a man's relationship to God.

Dispositional Distresses
Ecclesiastes 3:2-8

These verses point out where distresses are produced in a person's ordinary life and the part his disposition plays in them. Everything to do with a man's personal life, or with agricultural life, or with national life, is summed up in this chapter.

Personality and Ploughing
"A time to be born, and a time to die; a time to plant, and a time to pluck what is planted" (v. 2).

We cannot do anything without our ruling disposition instantly being marked in it. We gain our point of distress or of joy by the way we use or misuse our twenty-four hours.

Precious and Pernicious Healing

"A time to kill, and a time to heal; a time to break down, and a time to build up" (v. 3).

Every art, every healing, and every good, can be used for an opposite purpose. Every possibility I have of producing a fine character in time, I can use to produce the opposite; I have that liberty from the Creator. God will not prevent my disobeying Him; if He did, my obedience would not be worth anything. Some of us complain that God should have made the universe and human life like a foolproof machine, so simple that there would be no possibility of going wrong. If He had, we would have been like jellyfish. If there is no possibility of being damned, there is no need for salvation.

In the time between birth and death, most of us are in our "shell." There is something in us which makes us peck, and when the crack comes, instead if its being the gentle light and dawn of a new day, it is like a lightning flash. The universe we awaken to is not one of order, but a great big howling confusion, and it takes time to get adjusted. The distresses we reap in between God's decrees for us, we, together with other human beings, are personally responsible for. If we make our life a muddle, it is to a large extent because we have not discerned the great underlying relationship to God.

Priestesses of Death and Delight

"A time to weep, and a time to laugh; a time to mourn, and a time to dance" (v. 4).

Solomon runs a contrast between animal nature and human nature. Animals are guided by instinct; human beings are not. I may weave for myself what the Scots mean when they say, "Ye must dree yer weird." (You must endure your destiny or suffer your fate.) There is always a point where I have the power to choose whether or not I will take the consequences of my choice; no power to say whether or not I will be born; no power to choose my "cage." But within the cage I have power to choose which perch I will sit on. I cannot rule out the fact that between birth and death I have to choose. I have no power to act an act of pure will; to choose whether I will be born or not. But I have power to choose which way I will use the times as they come.

Solomon is indicating the times we make within God's time. This "time," this dispensation, is man's day, and in it we may do and say what we choose. Our talk may sound blatant, but we don't do much.

I can make my domestic life, my bodily life, and my agricultural life a priestess of sorrow or delight if I watch my disposition.

Pleasures and Pains—Domestic and Devotional

"A time to cast away stones, and a time to gather stones; a time to embrace, and a time to refrain from embracing" (v. 5).

Take Solomon in his profundities, and don't make him out to be a beast where he is an archangel. In the Song of Solomon he says an extraordinary thing which comes in like a refrain all through—"I charge you . . . do not stir up nor awaken love until it pleases." Many a man has awakened love before the time, and has reaped hell into the bargain. That "time" is in my power, but if I set myself to awaken love before I should, I may have all hell to live with instead of all heaven.

Profitless and Prosperous Commerce

"A time to gain, and a time to lose; a time to keep, and a time to throw away" (v. 6).

There comes a time when the only way to save what is of enormous value to life is to cast away all its possessions. "Your life will I give to you for a prey"—you will have nothing else, but you will escape with your life. There is a time when a man may have to lose everything he has got in order to save himself. (See Mark 8:35.)

Program of Speech and Silence
"A time to tear, and a time to sew; a time to keep silence, and a time to speak" (v. 7).

Sometimes it is cowardly to speak, and sometimes it is cowardly to keep silence. In the Bible the great test of a person's character is his tongue. (See James 1:26.) The tongue only came to its right place within the lips of the Lord Jesus Christ, because He never spoke from His right to Himself. He who was the wisdom of God incarnate, said, "The words that I speak to you I do not speak on My own authority," from the disposition of my right to Myself, but from My relationship to My Father. We are either too hasty or too slow; either we won't speak at all, or we speak too much, or we speak in the wrong mood. The thing that makes us speak is the lust to vindicate ourselves. ". . . leaving you an example . . . who committed no sin, nor was guile found in His mouth." Guile has the ingredient of self-vindication in it—My word, I'll make him smart for saying that about me! That spirit never was in Jesus Christ. The great deliverance for a man in time is to learn the program of speech and of silence.

Requited and Unrequited Love
"A time to love, and a time to hate; a time of war, and a time of peace" (v. 8).

The most painful and most crushing thing to a man or

woman is unrequited love. In summing up the attitude of men to Himself, God says that that is the way people treat Him, they "unrequite" His love. To most of us it is a matter of moonshine whether Jesus Christ lived or died or did anything at all; God has to "recommend" His love to us. (See Rom. 5:8, RSV.) It is only when we come to our wits' ends, or reap a distress, or feel the first twinge of damnation and are knocked out of our complacent mental agility over things, that we recognize the love of God.

Not one of these "times" are God's times, they are our times. For example, to call war either diabolical or divine is nonsense; war is human. War is a conflict of wills, not something that can be solved by law or philosophy. If you take what I want, you may talk till all's blue, either I will hit you or you'll hit me. It is no use to arbitrate when you get below into the elemental. In the time between birth and death this conflict of wills will go on until people by their relationship to God receive the disposition of the Son of God, which is holiness.

This is the Hebrew way of summing up in sentence after sentence all that makes an individual's life in time. Unless a person relates his disposition to God in between birth and death, he will reap a heritage of distress for himself and for those who come after him. The man who is banked on a real relationship to a personal God will reap not the distress that works death, but the joy of life.

Decrees of Despair
Ecclesiastes 2:9-10

"What profit has the worker from that in which he labors? I have seen the God-given task with which the sons of men are to be occupied."

"Honesty is the best policy," but immediately you are honest for that reason, you cease to be an honest man. "To be a good man means I shall be prosperous"; "to be rightly related to God means I shall be saved." All such considerations as these are beside the mark.

To terrorize someone into believing in God is never the work of God, but the work of human expediency. If we want to convince a congregation of a certain thing, we may use terror to frighten them into it; but never say that is God's way, it is our way. If we do not get conversions one way, then we preach hell fire and produce terror; we don't care what we preach as long as we dominate. To call that God's method is a travesty of the character of God. The methods God uses are indicated in Jesus Christ, and He never terrorized anyone. When He lifted the veil, He said, "How can you escape the damnation of hell?" The decrees of despair lie underneath everything a man does when once he rules out his relationship to God and takes rationalism as the basis of life. Solomon sums up the whole matter—unless a man is rightly related in confidence to God, everything he tries to do will end in despair.

Discretions of Deity
Ecclesiastes 3:11-15

Underlying everything we find the discretion and the wisdom of God.

Reasonableness

"He has made everything beautiful in its time. Also He has put eternity in their hearts, except that no one can find out the work that God does from beginning to end. I know that there is nothing better for them than to rejoice, and to do good in their lives, and also that every man should eat and drink and enjoy the good of all his labor—it is the gift of God" (vv. 11-13).

So that a man cannot in time find out the whole purpose of God. We begin by bringing Almighty God to the bar of judgment and saying—"Why did You make me?" "Who am I?" When we have done our jabbering and disputing we find that the implicit relationship of our personal life which we cannot get at, remains. Then we trace every kind of wisdom but find no direction in it, except in the wisdom of the Hebrews which reveals that the real fundamental relationship of our life is that of personal union with God. Until we get there, everything we are related to will go wrong.

"He has made everything beautiful in its time." And when God gets His time in you and in me, things will be beautiful again. The rationalist says that the only thing for a man to do is to live a reasonable life. A reasonable life and a philosophically rational life are totally different. Jesus Christ taught a reasonable life on the basis of faith in God—Be carefully careless about everything except your relationship to Me. Don't be disturbed today by thoughts about tomorrow, leave tomorrow alone, and bank in confidence on God's organization of what you do not see. Yesterday is past, there is no road back to it, tomorrow is not; live in the immediate present, and yours is the life of a child. God remakes things beautiful when He gets His time in us over again. In our "teens" we begin to get into the throes of life and we lose our sense of the beauty of things, and only after the throes when we get into a personal relationship with God do we find again that everything is beautiful. By means of our relationship to God we begin to find out how God works in our lives. In His time it comes, and we begin to spell out the character of God. "This is eternal life, that they may know You."

Rehabilitation

"I know that whatever God does, it shall be forever. Nothing can be added to it, and nothing taken from it. God does it, that men should fear before Him. That which is has already been, and what is to be has already been; and God requires an account of what is past" (vv. 14-15).

By the incarnate power of the Son of God, God rebuilds by degree the whole relationship of things, bringing every-thing back into oneness with Himself. That is the meaning of redemption—God has done His "bit." Sin is man's "bit." God's plan and design is not altered, but in the meantime man is countering it by his own design—We can bring it out in our own way. God is infinitely patient. He says over and over again—Not that way, My child, this is the way for you, a moral relationship to Myself. "He who is often reproved, and hardens his neck, will suddenly be destroyed, and that with-out remedy." God will not prevent my breaking my back; if He sees I am determined to go my own way, He won't stop me. But when my neck is broken, He lifts me up and moves me where He wants, no difficulty now. "The sacrifices of God are a broken spirit." When my heart is broken, the husk of individual relationship is merged into a personal relationship, and I find that God rehabilitates everything—He puts things back into their right fittings in me.

"There is nothing covered that will not be revealed, nor hidden that will not be known." There is no one who does not have some spot in his life where there is something dear, something that is a truth to him, a real, wonderful posses-sion full of light and liberty and joy, the finest spot in his experience. Jesus Christ says that ultimately through patience and by deliberately going on with God, everything that is now obscure will be as clear as that one spot. Will we "hang in" in patience? If we do, we shall see everything rehabilitated, and shall justify God in everything He has allowed.

Jesus Christ deliberately chose "the long, long trail"; we choose "the short cut," and continually go wrong until we understand the meaning of Psalm 23. "The Lord is my shepherd, He leads me in the right paths." It looked as if the way was leading nowhere but beside still waters and green pastures; but I begin to see that it is all unfolding one thing, that is, a personal relationship to God, which is the meaning of a man's life. The Bible declares that what is true in personal life will be true in material life; there will be "a new heaven and a new earth." The Utopian visions of socialists and atheists, dreamers and Christians, are all the same, there is no difference in their vision of a united human race, a perfect order of equity, everything in perfect harmony. But how is it to come about? We are all "in the soup" just now. No nation under heaven believes it is going to be brought about in Jesus Christ's way on the basis of redemption. We all believe it will be brought about by a line of things that has yet to be tried—socialism. We are on the verge of trying it, and it will be the nearest and the finest approach to fulfilling the vision; but at the point where it seems nearest fulfillment, it will make the biggest departure.[1]

---

[1] "The vision of socialism is magnificent; there are benedictions and blessings for mankind on the line of socialism which have never been yet; but if once the root is cut from redemption, it will be one of the most frantic forms of despotic tyranny the human race has ever known. It looks like the lamb, but when the big crisis comes, it gives life to the beast" (*The Shadow of an Agony,* p. 97. O.C.). This was stated by Oswald Chambers the year he died—the very year of the Russian Revolution in 1917. How prophetic he was!

Where did the Christ come from historically? From the people called the Jews. The blasphemy of a Gentile like Voltaire is futile; no Gentile can blaspheme, because no Gentile knows God in the way the Jew does. It takes the race that produced Jesus to produce Judas; and it will take the race that produced Christ to produce the antichrist. We are on the verge of this discovery. We are insular and closed in, and are looking in the wrong direction for the great big thing to come, instead of taking the Bible revelation. Abide in your relationship to God, and you will see that the "anti" comes on the same line as the positive.

In the Discipline of Discouragement
Ecclesiastes 3:16-22

"Glory of warrior, glory of orator, glory of song,
Paid with a voice flying by to the lost on an endless
    sea—
Glory of virtue, to fight, to struggle, to right the
    wrong—
Nay, but she aim'd not at glory, no lover of glory she:
Give her the glory of going on, and still to be.

The wages of sin is death; if the wages of Virtue be dust,
Would she have heart to endure for the life of the worm
    and the fly?
She desires no isles of the blest, no quiet seats of the
    just,
To rest in a golden grove, or to bask in a summer sky:
Give her the wages of going on, and not to die."

—Tennyson

"Discouragement is disenchanted egotism" (Mazzini). The heart knocked out of self-love. I expected things to go this way and they have not, so I shall give it all up.

The Perversion of Realized Ambition
Ecclesiastes 3:16

"Moreover I saw under the sun: in the place of judgment, wickedness was there; and in the place of righteousness, iniquity was there."

All through history we find it frequently happens that
when a man realizes his ambition, he turns it into diabolical
perversity right off the reel. In the Bible the conviction is
that the basis of human life is in the hand of God, not in the
hand of human reason, and that an exalted position, moral,
mental or spiritual, makes an individual either more God-like
or more devil-like, and that by the decree of God and not by
chance. When a man has mounted high and has the satisfaction of having fulfilled his ambition, he is compelled to be
either a great humble person or a diabolical fiend. Solomon is
pointing out that when a man realizes his ambition, he may
pervert it and become tyrannical. Unless kings and rulers are
God-fearing, they may become tyrants of the wildest order.

One of the great stirring truths of the Bible is that the
man who looks for justice from others is a fool. In moral and
spiritual life if a man has a sense of injustice, he ceases to be
of value to his fellowmen. Never waste your time looking for
justice; if you do you will soon put yourself in bandages and
give way to self-pity. Our business is to see that no one suffers from our injustice.

The man who has satisfied his ambition may suddenly
become a miserable tyrant and all his joy will go. "These
things I have spoken to you," said Jesus, "that My joy may
remain in you." What joy did Jesus have? He failed appar-
ently in everything He came to do; all His disciples forsook
Him, He was crucified, and yet He talked of His joy. The
joy of our Lord lay in doing what the Father sent Him to do.

His purpose was not to succeed, but to fulfill the design of His coming—"For I have come down from heaven, not to do My own will, but the will of Him who sent Me."

What is the real design of man's creation? Solomon deals with every possible phase of life—metaphysics, philosophy, religion, commercial prosperity, moral integrity—not as guesswork, he had been through it all. No one has the wisdom of Solomon and his verdict is that it all ends in disaster. That is the summing up of it all unless a man sees that his "chief end is to glorify God and enjoy Him forever," and it takes a long while to get there. To put things on any other basis will end in disaster.

The Prevailing of Righteous Authority
Ecclesiastes 3:17

"I said in my heart, 'God shall judge the righteous and the wicked, for there shall be a time there for every purpose and for every work.'"

"God shall judge the righteous and the wicked." But who is God? I have never seen God, or spoken to Him. An omnipresent, omniscient, omnipotent Being does not amount to anything to me; He is an abstract finding of a man's intellect. Can God take on hands and feet and man's ways of doing things, and manifest Himself on the plane on which we live? The Bible says that that is what God did do. Jesus Christ lived a human life on this earth, and He exhibited a disposition which was not yours and not mine. Any man who does not deceive himself knows perfectly well that he has not a disposition like Jesus Christ's. We have only to read the Sermon on the Mount and see God's demand for a fathomlessly pure heart, to know that. What Jesus Christ exhibited was not omnipotence and omniscience and omnipresence, but absolute holiness in human flesh, and He said "he who has seen Me has seen the Father." Jesus Christ is the judge. "The Father . . . has committed all judgment to the Son" (John 5:22).

Would I be concerned if my "buddy" were handed over to Jesus Christ to be judged, handed over to the Being who paid the price of redemption, who lived the spell of God's dispensation between birth and death on the plane on which we live, and manifested an unsulliedly holy life, the Being who claims He can put His own disposition into me, the One who says, "I am the first and the last," the One to whom all judgment has been given? Or would I be prepared to trust His honor and stake everything on Him?

We cannot judge ourselves by ourselves or by anyone else. There is always one fact more in everyone's life that we do not know. We cannot put men into types, we are never at the balance of one another's heredity; therefore the judg-ment cannot lie with us. Solomon says that God's judgment is right and true and that a man can rest his heart there. It is a great thing to notice the things we cannot answer just now, and to waive our judgment about them. Because you cannot explain a thing, don't say there is nothing in it. There are dark and mysterious and perplexing things in life, but the prevailing authority at the back of all is a righteous authority, and a man does not need to be unduly concerned. When we do find out the judgment of God, we shall be absolutely sat-isfied with it to the last degree, we won't have another word to say—"that You may be found just when You speak, and blameless when You judge."

In the meantime God has something from which to clear His character when we see Him—"and God will wipe away every tear from their eyes." There is no problem, no personal grief, no agony or distress (and God knows there are some fathomless agonies just now—awful injustices and wrongs and evils and nobility all mixed up together), but will have an overwhelming explanation one day. If we will hang in to the fact that God is true and loving and just, every judgment He passes will find us in agreement with it finally.

Solomon is saying from his pre-incarnation standpoint that every man when he sees the judgment of God untramelled by bodily limitations, will say that God was perfectly right in all He allowed. Can any one of us say now that God's character is clear? It is ridiculous to pin our faith to a creed about God. The experience of Job is a proof that creeds must go. Every now and again we have to outgrow our creeds. Morally it is better to be an atheist than to believe in a God whom "to be God is not fit."

The Parallel of Perishableness
Ecclesiastes 3:18-21

"I said in my heart, 'Concerning the estate of the sons of men, God tests them, that they may see that they them-selves are like beasts.' For what happens to the sons of men also happens to beasts; one thing befalls them: as one dies, so dies the other. Surely, they all have one breath; man has no advantage over beasts, for all is vanity. All go to one place: all are from the dust, and all return to dust. Who knows the spirit of the sons of men, which goes upward, and the spirit of the beast, which goes down to the earth?"

There is a philosophy which says that if a man wills it, he need never die; but he cannot will it! There is a limit to will; no one can will pure will. Solomon is saying you may do what you like, but you will die like a dog. He is dealing with the spell of our actual lives; we all die. It is humiliating for our predications to remember that although the spirit of man is indestructible, the phase of life which we bank on naturally passes. We may have labor in it, and delight and satisfaction in it, but it will all pass. When a beast dies, his body disappears and his soul goes downward into entire nature. The spirit of man goes straight back to God who made it; it is never absorbed into God.

The essence of Christianity is not adherence to principles but a personal relationship to God through Jesus Christ at work in the whole of my life. The people who influence us are not those who set out to do it, they are prigs. But the folk who have a real relationship to God and who never bother whether they are being of use—these are a continual assistance.

The Probation of Reasonable Activity
Ecclesiastes 3:22

"So I perceived that there is nothing better than that a man should rejoice in his own works, for that is his heritage. For who can bring him to see what will happen after him?"

The basis of things is not rational. Reason is our guide among facts but reason cannot explain facts. Reason and logic and intellect have to do with the time between birth and death, but they can give no explanation of before birth or after death. All we infer of either is speculation; it may be interesting but it is apt to blind us to true facts. Solomon deals with the expression of practical life as it is, and he finds it a sorry mess. He says it is a philosophic plaster to say that when someone gives up a thing he makes it easier for those who come after him; a man does not find his true joy in sacrificing or in sin or in labor. We may be laying the foundations for those who come after us, but "who can bring him to see what will happen after him?" It sounds all right, but is there any enjoyment in it? True enjoyment is not in what we do but in our relationships. If a man is true to God, everything between birth and death will work out on the line of joy. If we bank in what we do, whether it is good or bad, we are off the track. The one thing that matters is personal relationship.

What, then, are we to do in our ordinary active life? It is not a question of making it easy for those who come after us, but of what a man is to do in the spell between birth and death. According to our Lord's teaching, a man has to base his life on his relationship to God and live according to that relationship with the simple gaiety of a child. If we apply the Sermon on the Mount to our ideas of individual and national life we shall find how we ignore what our Lord teaches. Wherever Christianity comes straight home to us, we ignore it; when it gets at others, we preach it for all we are worth. The general history of Christianity is that it has been tried and abandoned because it is found to be difficult; but wherever it has been tried and honorably gone on with, it has never failed.

Our civilization is based on the foundation of murder—the first civilization was founded by Cain; and civilized life is a vast, complicated, more or less gilded-over system of murder. This does not mean that civilization can never be just and right. The Bible speaks of a "holy city," "a new earth," and reveals that it is to be brought about by the man who lives his life based on God in all his relationships and does not worry about what he is going to do later.

When we study Hebrew wisdom we see how terrifically far we have degenerated away from God and from confidence in God. Nowadays the almighty microbe has blotted God out of his heaven. When we come to the "soup" we are in just now, the catastrophic earthquake that is blasting the whole globe to bits, all we can do is to put on plasters and borrow opportunist phrases. According to Hebrew wisdom, the thing to do is to bank on our faith in God, and where our duty lies do it like a man "and damn the consequences."

When in doubt physically, dare. When in moral doubt, stop. When in spiritual doubt, pray. And when in personal doubt, be guided by your life with God. Base all on God, and slowly and surely the actual life will be educated along the particular line of your relationship to Him.

On Winking the Other Eye
Ecclesiastes 4

"Why do they prate of the blessings of Peace? we have made them a curse,
Pickpockets, each hand lusting for all that is not its own;
And lust of gain, in the spirit of Cain, is it better or worse
Than the heart of the citizen hissing in war on his own hearthstone?

Sooner or later I too may passively take the print
Of the golden age—why not? I have neither hope nor trust;
May make my heart as a millstone, set my face as a flint,
Cheat and be cheated, and die; who knows? we are ashes and dust."

— Tennyson

The title of this chapter indicates the treachery that there is in you and in me, and consequently in others! One of the first things to develop in a child is the realization that he can "do" something.

Solomon will not allow us to imagine that life is other than full of cunning and craft and deception. The "babe in the woods" idea does not hold—"I don't know how he could do it!" Not one of us has a single motive; the only One who had a single motive was Jesus Christ, and the miracle of His redemption is that He can put a single motive into any man. There is no cunning in the Sermon on the Mount. As long as we deal on the line of craft and cunning, Jesus Christ is no good to us. We can easily make a fool of goodness. The romance of the life of a disciple is not an external fascination but an inner martyrdom.

Tennyson and Browning and Carlyle all write as men who see things without the glamour of temperament or religion or conceit. To look at life as it is, and to think of it as it is, must make a man a pessimist. If we are not pessimistic, it is either because we are generally thick-headed and do not think, or because we have temperaments that are optimistic. If we face things as they are, we shall find that true optimism comes from a source other than temperament. According to Solomon, it comes from applying Hebrew wisdom. Today we are bothered over finding out whether there is a God and what is the origin of things. Solomon faces facts as they are.

The Oppression of Tyranny
Ecclesiastes 4:1-3

"Then I returned and considered all the oppression that is done under the sun: And look! The tears of the oppressed, but they have no comforter—on the side of their oppressors there was power, but they have no comforter. Therefore I praised the dead who were already dead, more than the living who are still alive. Yet, better than both is he who has never existed, who has not seen the evil work that is done under the sun."

In this chapter Solomon deals with injustice and tyranny; over-reaching and craftiness. Verses 1-3 are a statement of things as they are. The spell between birth and death is mine, and I along with other human beings make the kind of life I live. I cannot make it independently of other wills, unless I happen to be a Napoleon or a Kaiser and bind my will on everything under my power.

The oppression of tyranny means that I drive my will on other people, and if they do not do what I want, I break them. It is an oppression in which one power crushes another. "The tears of such as were oppressed"—nothing can heal them. Think of the devastations and havoc throughout the world just now. What is going to make up to the people who are broken? To say that "every cloud has a silver lining" is a kind lie. Unless we can get into a relationship with the God whom the Bible reveals, life is not worth living. Most of us are mercifully shielded, we are not sensitive enough to feel or to experience the terrific things that Solomon experienced and saw in his lifetime; we see things through colored, or cynical, glasses, but the cynic's standpoint is not a true one, it distorts things.

In human life as it is, the oppression of tyranny has the biggest run. Take the things we experience out of our own circle where they are balanced by domestic affections, into a setting where these things do not count, and see if Solomon is drawing a long bow. Jesus Christ in His day submitted to the providential order of tyranny represented by Pilate (see Jn. 18:36; 19:10,11). He saw that tyranny was inevitable because the nation to which He belonged had fallen from the standard it should have lived up to.

"And God will wipe away every tear from their eyes." There will come one day a personal and direct touch from God when every tear and perplexity, every oppression and distress, every suffering and pain, and wrong and injustice will have a complete and ample and overwhelming explanation. The Christian faith is exhibited by the man who has the spiritual courage to say that that is the God he trusts in, and it takes some moral backbone to do it. It is easier to attempt to judge everything in the span between birth and death.

The Oppression of Trade
Ecclesiastes 4:4

"Again, I saw that for all toil and every skillful work a man is envied by his neighbor. This also is vanity and grasping for the wind."

If you go back to the origin of civilization, you find it was founded by a murderer. Among the good things, the shielding and protecting things, that are the outcome of civilization, what Solomon mentions is always to be found—the crushing of someone in order to get gain. It may be done kindly or brutally, but the basis of success must be the crushing of something or someone. There is a rivalry between men, and we have made it a good thing; we have made ambition and competition the very essence of civilized life. No wonder there is no room for Jesus Christ, and no room for the Bible. We are all so scientifically orthodox nowadays, so materialistic and certain that rationalism is the basis of things, that we make the Bible out to be the most revolutionary, unorthodox and heretical of books. Jesus Christ echoes Solomon's attitude: "For a man's life does not consist in the abundance of the things which he possesses."

At the basis of trade and civilized life lie oppression and tyranny. Whether you are king or subject, says Solomon, you cannot find joy in any system of civilized life, or in trade or commerce; for underneath there is a rivalry that stings and bites, and the kindest man will put his heel on his greatest friend. These are not the blind statements of a disappointed man, but statements of facts discerned by the wisest man that ever lived.

The Oppression of Idling
Ecclesiastes 4:5-6

"The fool folds his hands and consumes his own flesh. Better is a handful with quietness than both hands full, together with toil and grasping for the wind."

"The best thing to do is to be a Bohemian and have nothing to do with civilized life; to live from hand to mouth and not do a hand's turn." This has been a cult in every age of civilized life. We have seen it in our own day in Charles Wagner and his plea for a simple life, and in Walt Whitman and Thoreau, who advocated the simple life on a higher line. When a man is fed up with a certain line of things, he revolts and goes to the opposite extreme. Today tyranny and oppression have eaten into man's sense of justice, and they have revolted and gone to the other extreme.

Solomon tried first of all to get at the secret of things through philosophy and thinking; then he revolted into a reign of animal passion; then as king he insisted on good laws, but found he was oppressing the life out of the people; then he realized the tyranny of trade and tried idling, but found that that too oppressed.

In all trade and commerce there is oppression, and we try to justify it by saying that the weakest must go to the wall. But is that so? Where are the mighty civilizations of other days? Where are the prehistoric animals, those colossal powerful creatures? It is they that have gone to the wall. The great blunder in all kingdoms among men is that we will demand strong men, consequently each kingdom in its turn goes to the wall because no chain is stronger than its weakest link. Jesus Christ founded His Kingdom on the weakest link of all—a baby. "Marvel not that I said unto you, you must be born again." Consequently the gates of hell cannot prevail against His Kingdom.

The Obsession of Solitariness
Ecclesiastes 4:7-8

"Then I returned, and I saw vanity under the sun: There is one alone, without companion: He has neither son nor brother. Yet there is no end to all his labors, nor is his eye satisfied with riches. But he never asks, 'For whom do I toil and deprive myself of good?' This also is vanity and a grave misfortune."

There is such a thing as an obsession of solitariness. Hermits, ascetics, and celibates cut themselves off in revolt—"Because I cannot find peace or joy or happiness in the tyranny of civilized life or in commerce, and I cannot be an idle tramp, I become a solitary and live a sequestered life." Solomon points out what history has proven—that this is an experiment that ends disastrously, because a man cannot shut out what is inside by cutting himself off from the outside. Jesus Christ was not a solitary man—"The Son of Man has come eating and drinking, and you say, Look, a glutton and a winebibber, a friend of tax collectors and sinners!" John the Baptist was a solitary man—"For John the Baptist came neither eating bread nor drinking wine, and you say, he has a demon."

"Oh, that I had wings like a dove! For then I would fly away and be at rest." The desire is to be solitary—"If only I could get away and be quiet; if only I could live in a sunrise or a sunset!" We have to find our true life in things as they are with that on the inside which keeps us right. The true energy of life lies in being rightly related to God, and only there is true joy found.

It is an interesting study in psychology to watch people who are engaged in drastic social and rescue work and find out whether they are doing it for a surcease from their own troubles, to get relief from a broken heart. In a great many cases the worker wants a plaster for his own life. He takes up slum work, not because it is the great passion of his life, but because he must get something to deliver him from the gnawing pain of his own heart. The people he works among are often right when they say he is doing it to save his own soul.

The Optimism of Society
Ecclesiastes 4:9-12

"Two are better than one, because they have a good reward for their labor. For if they fall, one will lift up his companion. But woe to him who is alone when he falls, for he has no one to help him up. Again, if two lie down together, they will keep warm; but how can one be warm alone? Though one may be overpowered by another, two can withstand him. And a threefold cord is not quickly broken."

The conclusion that Solomon comes to is that trade is better than idling; that both solitariness and society as it is are pretty bad, but that society is better than solitariness. Domestic life and married life and comradeship are all advocated by Solomon. (See 1 Tim. 5:1-3.) The Bible always emphasizes the facts of life as they are. Whenever Jesus Christ applied His teaching to actual life He focused it round two points—marriage and money. If the religion of

Jesus Christ and the indwelling of the Spirit of God cannot deal with these things and keep a man and woman as God wants them to be, His religion is useless.

The Occasion of Sagacity and Stubbornness
Ecclesiastes 4:13-16

"Better is a poor and wise youth than an old and foolish king who will be admonished no more. For he comes out of prison to be king, although he was born poor in his kingdom. I saw all the living who walk under the sun; they were with the second youth who stands in his place. There was no end of all the people over whom he was made king; yet those who come afterward will not rejoice in him. Surely this also is vanity and grasping for the wind."

It is a disastrous thing for a man never to be ragged, an appalling thing to be a privileged young man! A lad who has been his mother's pet and has been brought up like a hot-house plant is totally unprepared for the scathing of life as it is, and when he is flung out into the rugged realities of life, he suffers intolerably. Conceive the suffering of a lad who has been sheltered, never had anything go against him, never been thwarted, when the tension does come. It is better to be a wise youth who can stand being ragged and taken down. One can always recognize the lad who has not been with others, he will not be admonished, consequently you cannot warn him.

Solomon says whether you are wise or foolish, upright or not, a king or tyrannized over by a king, successful or a failure, in society or solitary, stubborn or sagacious, all alike end the same way. All is passing, and we cannot find our lasting joy in any element we like to touch. It is disastrous for a man to try and find true joy in any phase of truth, or in the fulfillment of ambition, or in physical or intellectual solitariness, or in society; he will find his joy only in a personal relationship with God. That relationship was expounded by Jesus Christ when He said, "If anyone comes to Me and does not hate his father and mother, wife and children, brothers and sisters, yes, and his own life also, he cannot be My disciple." Our first concern is to be personally related to God. Jesus Christ is God manifested in human flesh, and we have to ignore to the point of hatred anything that competes with our relationship to Him.

When once a man is there, he receives a hundredfold more of all he gave up to get there, and he never demands an infinite satisfaction from those other relationships. The man or woman who does not know God demands an infinite satisfaction from other human beings which they cannot give, and in the case of the man, he becomes tyrannical and cruel. It springs from this one thing, the human heart must have satisfaction, but there is only one Being who can satisfy the last abyss of the human heart, and that is the Lord Jesus Christ. When once a man or woman is rightly related to Him, the one never demands the impossible from the other, everything is in its right place. "If anyone desires to come after Me, let him deny himself," that is, deny his right to himself. The essence of sin is self-realization, my prideful right to myself. The disposition that ought to rule is God's right to me, Christ-realization.

It takes a long time for any one of us to realize our need of Jesus Christ personally, and it takes a nation a long time to realize that the only way things can be put right is not on the basis of rationalism, but only on the basis of redemption. The Bible is neither obsolete nonsense nor poetic blether: It is a universe of revelation facts.

A Man's Reach
Should Exceed His Grasp
Ecclesiastes 5:1-7

"Glory about thee, without thee;
And thou fulfillest thy doom
Making Him broken gleams,
And a stifled splendor and gloom,

Speak to Him thou for He hears,
And Spirit with Spirit can meet—
Closer is He than breathing,
And nearer than hands and feet."

—Tennyson

If we try to find lasting joy in any human relationship it will
end in vanity, something that passes like a morning cloud.
The true joy of a man's life is in his relationship to God, and
the great point of the Hebrew confidence in God is that it
does not unfit a man for his actual life. That is always the
test of a false religion.

The Rectitude of Ritualism
Ecclesiastes 5:1

"Walk prudently when you go to the house of God; and draw near to hear rather than to give the sacrifice of fools, for they do not know that they do evil."

There is a use for ritual in a man's religious life. Because a thing is necessary at one time of life, it does not follow that it is necessary all through. There may be times when ritual is a good thing and other times when it is not. Bear in mind that in the Hebrew religion there is an insistence on ecclesiasticism and ritual. In the New Testament that is finished with (see John 4:21-24); but Ezekiel prophesies that the true worship of God will yet be established on earth as it has never yet been, and there will be ritual then to an extraordinary degree.

In the present day the revolt is against ritual and form; with the average man ritual is at a discount. There is a time in a healthy religious when the revolt is right. In the history of the salvation of a man's soul it may be better to worship in a whitewashed building, with a bare rugged simplicity of service; but while it is true that a man may go through forms and ceremonies and be a downright hypocritical humbug, it is also true that he may despise ritual and be as big a humbug. When we are in a right relationship to God ritual is an assistance; the place of worship and the atmosphere are both conducive to worship. We are apt to ignore the fact that ritual is essential in a full-orbed religious life, that there is a rectitude in worship only brought about by the right use of ritual. For instance, when Jesus Christ taught His disciples to pray, He gave them a form of prayer which He knew would be repeated through the Christian centuries.

A Man's Reach Should Exceed His Grasp 65

The Rashness of Reaction vs. Recollectedness of Religion
Ecclesiastes 5:2

"Do not be rash with your mouth, and let not your heart utter anything hastily before God. For God is in heaven, and you on earth; therefore let your words be few."

When you have been through a bereavement, or have thought you would be found out in a wrong and were not, there is the danger of reacting into a rash spell of devotion. You read your Bible and say things to God, but there is no reality in it. It is like the reaction of a man after a drinking bout, he mistakes his remorse for repentance. Repentance is not a reaction, remorse is. Remorse is—I will never do the thing again. Repentance is that I deliberately become the opposite to what I have been.

Solomon says—Beware of this kind of religiousness; don't be rash with your mouth, hold yourself in. When you go into the presence of God, remember it is not to be in a passing mood; everything we say to God is recognized by God and held clear in our record. Solomon indicates that it is better to have nothing to do with religious life than to talk religion in rashness only. "These are the ones . . . when they hear the word, immediately receive it with gladness; and they have no root in themselves, and so endure only for a time."

In war, there is less of the rashness of reaction than might be supposed; it has rather been the opposite way. Many a man has had the "bivvers" (that is, a mixture of fear and cowardice and a determination to go through) has said, "I feel inclined to look at my Bible; but no, I haven't read it before and I won't now." Again, a man may suddenly in the rashness of reaction pretend he is religious; but there is nothing in it. The characteristic of true religion is recollect-edness; pull yourself together, stop wool-gathering, and remember that you are in the presence of God.

The Refrainings of Reverence
Ecclesiastes 5:3

"For a dream comes through much activity, and a fool's voice is known by his many words."

If you are busy in your daily life, the dreams you have at night may be simply the refractions of the "multitude of business." Any amount of futile religion is based on this line of things—"I have been eating too much, but now Lent has come and I will fast for a time." There is nothing genuine in it, it has not the grip of God about it. When a man comes into the presence of God he refrains himself and remembers that he is not there to suffer from his own reactions, to get comfort for himself, to pray along the line of "O Lord, bless me." He is there to refrain from his own personal needs and to get into the scope of God's outlook.

The Repudiation of Responsibility
Ecclesiastes 5:4-6

"When you make a vow to God, do not delay to pay it; for He has no pleasure in fools. Pay what you have vowed. It is better not to vow than to vow and not pay. Do not let your mouth cause your flesh to sin, nor say before the mes-senger of God that it was an error. Why should God be angry at your excuse and destroy the work of your hands?"

At the end of the year we hear much about vowing. Solomon's advice is—Don't vow, for if you make a vow even in ordinary matters and do not keep it, you are the worse for it. If you make an engagement to meet a man and don't fulfill it, you suffer for it. It will mean a defect in your general make-up. It is better not to promise, better to be uncertain, than to promise and not fulfill. We are all apt to be like Rip Van Winkle and say—"I won't count this time." We reap terrific damage to our own characters when we vow and do not perform. You may not take account of the fact that you made an engagement and did not keep it; but your nerves do, the record is there. Solomon's counsel in practical life as well as in religious life is—never make a vow unless at all costs you carry it through. Promises are a way of shirking responsibility. We can get over an unpleasant interview by promising to do a thing; but it is an appalling thing to say "Yes, I will," and then not do it. Don't pile up vows before men, and certainly not before God.

Jesus Christ was stern along this line. "No one, having put his hand to the plow, and looking back, is fit for the kingdom of God." When Hezekiah was sick he vowed a vow before God—"I shall go softly" ("as in a solemn procession," RSV, marg.), "all my years." But when he was out of danger he forgot all about his vow. To face death day in and day out, as men do in war, is a different matter from facing sickness or an accident. If you have had a narrow escape and have come through, don't be rash in reaction; don't promise and make vows, but look to God and bank on the reality of Jesus Christ.

One of the dangers in modern evangelism is that it lays the emphasis on decision for Christ instead of on surrender to Jesus Christ. That to me is a grave blunder. When a man decides for Christ he usually puts his confidence in his own honor, not in Christ at all. No man can keep himself a Christian, it is impossible; it is God who keeps a man a Christian. Many a man is kept away from Jesus Christ by honesty—"I won't be able to keep it up."

If Christianity depends on decisions for Christ, it is better to keep away from it; but our Lord tells us to come to Him because we are not able to decide—a very different proposition. Jesus Christ came for the weak, for the ungodly and the sinful, and He says, "Blessed are the poor in spirit," not—"Blessed is the man who has the power to decide and to keep his vow." Jesus Christ calls the man who says, "I cannot do it; others may have the strength, but I haven't." Jesus Christ says to such, "Blessed are you." It is not our vows before God that tell, but our coming before God, exactly as we are in all our weakness, and being held and kept by God.

Recklessness vs. Resoluteness of Righteousness
Ecclesiastes 5:7

"For in the multitude of dreams and many words there is also vanity. But fear God."

There is such a thing as being haunted on the inside of the life. It begins when a man tampers with the borders of spiritualism and communicates with supernatural powers; he opens the unconscious part of his personality to all kinds of powers he cannot control. The only cure is to fear God, to be rightly related to God, and these fears and hauntings will go. "Put on the whole armor of God."

When a man is related to God through Jesus Christ, God protects not only the conscious life but the unconscious life as well. Unless a man is guarded by God, there are forces that can find their way into the unconscious domain. There are dreams and influences that tamper with a man's life and leave him a haunted man. No man has any right to make curiosity, which is his guide in intellectual life, his guide in moral life. No man ever does it without falling. It is a terrible thing to be haunted, to have your own conscience laugh at you.

When we are related to God, He guards from dangers seen and unseen. The man who fears God has nothing else to fear, he is guarded in his conscious and unconscious life, in his waking and his sleeping moments.

The Triune—
Dust, Drudgery, Deity
Ecclesiastes 5:8-20

"Ah, make the most of what we yet may spend,
Before we too into the Dust descend;
 Dust into Dust, and under Dust to lie
Sans Wine, sans Song, sans Singer, and—sans End!

Alike for those who for Today prepare,
And those that after a Tomorrow stare,
 A *muezzin* from the Tower of Darkness cries,
'Fools! your reward is neither Here nor There.'"

—Omar Khayyam

God made man a mixture of dust and Deity—"And the Lord
God formed man of the dust of the ground, and breathed into
his nostrils the breath of life; and man became a living being"
(Gen. 2:7). The dust of a man's body is his glory, not his
shame. Jesus Christ manifested Himself in that dust, and He
claims that He can presence any man with His own divinity.
The New Testament teaches us how to keep the body under
and make it a servant. Robert Browning, of all the poets, is
the one who insists that we make headway not in spite of

71

the flesh, but because of the flesh, and in no other way.

Drudgery is the outcome of sin, but it has no right to be the rule of life. It becomes the rule of life because we ignore the fact that the dust of the earth belongs to God, and that our chief end is to glorify God. Unless we can maintain the presence of Divinity in our dust, life becomes a miserable drudgery. If we live in order to hoard up the means of living, we do not live at all, we have no time to, we are taken up with one form of drudgery or another to keep things going.

The wisdom of today concerns itself chiefly with the origin of things and not with God, consequently neither the philosopher nor the mystic has time for actual life. The wisdom of the Hebrews concerns itself with practical life, and recognizes that the basis of things is tragic. The Bible attitude to practical life is at a discount with most of us because we are far away from the rooted and grounded confidence in the God of the Hebrews.

We do not think on Bible lines, we think on pagan lines, and only in our emotional life do we dabble in spirituality; consequently when we are hard hit, our religion finds us dumb; or if we do talk, we talk as pagans. It has been fashionable to have a contempt for anyone who believes in the Book of Genesis. But now the war has hit us a fair blow and we cannot talk so glibly, nor are we so certain that our cocksureness about things is right; we are not so insolent in our attitude to the Bible standpoint. We are beginning to be prepared to think.

The Bible has no sympathy with saying things ought not to be as they are. The practical thing is to look at things as they are. What is the use of saying there ought to be no war, in the meantime there is! There ought to be no injustice, there is! There ought to be no violence, there is! Solomon never wastes his time in that way; he says these things are. We can ignore facing them, or we can face them in a way which will lead us either to despair or to the cross of Jesus Christ.

Providential Order of Tyranny
Ecclesiastes 5:8

"If you see the oppression of the poor, and the violent perversion of justice and righteousness in a province, do not marvel at the matter; for high official watches over high official, and higher officials are over them."

All through the Bible the difference between God's order and God's permissive will is brought out. God's permissive will is the things that are now, whether they are right or wrong. If you are looking for justice, you will come to the conclusion that God is the devil; and if the providential order of things today were God's order, then that conclusion would be right. But if the order of things today is God's permissive will, that is quite another matter.

God's order is no sin, no Satan, no wrong, no suffering, no pain, no death, no sickness, and no limitation; God's providential will is the haphazard things that are on just now in which we have to fight and make character in, or else be damned by. We may kick and yell and say God is unjust, but we are all "in the soup." It is no use saying things are not as they are; it is no use being amazed at the providential order of tyranny, it is there. In personal life and in national life God's order is reached through pain, and never in any other way. Why it should be so is another matter, but that it is so obvious. ". . . though He was a Son, yet He learned obedience by the things which He suffered."

We have to get hold of God's order in the midst of His permissive will. God is bringing many "sons" to glory. A son is more than a saved soul; a son is one who has been through the fight and stood the test and come out sterlingly worthy. The Bible attitude to things is absolutely robust, there is not the tiniest whine about it; there is no possibility of lying like a limp jellyfish on God's providence, it is never allowed for a second. There is always a sting and a kick all through the Bible.

Solomon says when you see the providential order of tyranny, don't be amazed at it. According to the Bible the explanation is that the basis of things is tragic; things have gone wrong and they can only be put right and brought into God's order by the individual relationship of men and women. We find tyranny everywhere. Take it in a personal way—we all think we are the creatures of injustice. There never was a man who was not! Justice is an abstraction at the back of our heads. It is absurd to make abstractions entities.

Justice and righteousness are emanations from a personal God, and it is His presence and ruling that gives these abstractions their meaning. We say that God is just—where is the evidence of it? Jesus Christ taught, "From him who wants to borrow from you do not turn away"—where is the justice in that? The great lasting point is not an abstraction called justice, not a question of right or wrong, of goodness or badness, but a personal relationship to a personal God. If I expect to see everything in the universe good and right and I find it is not, I get faint-hearted. Solomon won't have us go off on the limbo of the abstract and say these things ought not to be; they are! Injustice and lust and rapine and murder and crime and bestiality and grabbing are as thick as desert sand, and it is cowardly for a man to say because things are as they are, therefore he must drift. We say we had to take a particular course because the prevailing trend of God's providence was that way. It is a remarkable thing that two boats can sail in opposite directions in the same wind, they can go according to the steering skill of the pilot and not according to the prevailing wind; and in the same way a man can trim his sails and grasp hold of God's order however much it costs him.

We need to be warned against the books that pander to our weak side, and the folks who say — "Poor fellow, he couldn't help it." It may be a kindly thing to say, but some things should not be treated with kindness. There is a tyrannic order which runs all through life, and if we get slopped over with sentiment, we are not only unfit for life, but are of no use whatever to lay hold of God's order in the midst of things as they are. If the incarnation means anything to a man, it means fight, "with breast and back as either should be," indwelt by the Spirit of God. Beware of the things that are apt to lead you to a side eddy — false spirituality or intellectual contempt will do it.

Profit Ordained of Tillage
Ecclesiastes 5:9

"Moreover the profit of the land is for all; the king himself is served from the field."

When God created man He made him of dust and Deity; sin introduced the other element — drudgery. "Cursed is the ground for your sake; in toil you shall eat of it all the days of your life. Both thorns and thistles it shall bring forth for you . . . . In the sweat of your face you shall eat bread." The earth is cursed because of man's apostasy, and when that apostasy ceases in actual history, the ground will no longer bring forth the curse. The final redemption includes "new heavens and a new earth." Instead of the thorn shall come up the cypress tree;" and "the wolf also shall dwell with the lamb." Instead of the savage ferocity of the beasts, there will be the strength without the savageness—an inconceivable order of things just now.

In anything like a revolution or a war, we find what Solomon refers to here is true, that to make profit you must go back to the dust you came from. The curious thing about civilization is that it tends to take men away from the soil, and makes them develop an artificial existence away from the elemental. Civilization has become an elaborate way of doing without God, and when civilized life is hit a smashing blow by any order of tyranny, most of us have not a leg to stand on. Solomon reminds us that king and peasant alike can only gain their profit by proper tillage of the soil. The laws given in the Bible include a scheme for the treatment of the earth and they insist on proper rest being given to the land, and make it clear that that alone will bring profit in actual existence. Leviticus 25 is the great classic on the rights of the earth.

Profitless Possession of Treasure
Ecclesiastes 5:10-11

"He who loves silver will not be satisfied with silver; nor he who loves abundance, with increase. This also is vanity. When goods increase, they increase who eat them; so what profit have the owners except to see them with their eyes?"

To make treasure is different from making profit. Treasure is the thing that is esteemed for itself, not for what it brings. The Bible tirades against possession for possession's sake. "Lay up for yourselves treasures in heaven, . . . for where your treasure is, there your heart will be also." If your treasure is in gold or in land or the possessions of earth, that is where your heart will be, and when wars and rumors of wars arise, your heart will fail you for fear. If a man has his treasure vested in bonds and a war strikes, how can he keep his mind at rest? Panic and devastation and ruin are the result—profitless in every degree.

The manipulation of civilized life has not resulted in the development of the tillage of the land, but in the building up of treasure, and it is not only the miser who grabs. The sense of possession is a snare to true spiritual life. Paul uses the life of a soldier to illustrate a saint's life (see 2 Tim. 2:3-4). No sense of property or possession can go along with an abiding detachment. In civilized life it is the building up of possessions that is the snare—This is *my* house, *my* land; these are *my* books, and *my* things—imagine when they are touched! I am consumed with distress. Over and over again Jesus Christ drives this point home—Remember, don't have your heart in your possessions, let them come and go. Solomon warns about the same thing—whatever possessions you have will consume the nobility of the life in an appalling way. In the case of Job, Satan asked permission to play havoc with his possessions and God gave him permission, and every possession Job had, even to his bodily health, went; but Job proved that a man would remain true to his love of God though all his possessions went to rack and ruin.

Peace Out of Toil
Ecclesiastes 5:12

"The sleep of a laboring man is sweet, whether he eats little or much; but the abundance of the rich will not permit him to sleep."

"The sleep of a laboring man is sweet"; it recreates him.

The Bible indicates that sleep is not meant only for the recuperation of a man's body, but that there is a tremendous furtherance of spiritual and moral life during sleep. The conception of sleep that any practical man has is that we need just enough to recuperate the body. According to the Bible, a great deal more than physical recuperation happens in the sleep of any man who has done his daily toil in actual work. "He giveth to his beloved in sleep" (Ps. 127:2 RSV). This is a phase that is cut out altogether, because we ignore the deeper issues.

"Whether he eats little or much." Paul's counsel is that "if any would not work, neither should he eat." There are plenty of folks who eat but don't work, and they suffer for it. We are physically healthy, the benefit of the food we eat corresponds to the work we do, and the same is true in mental, moral and spiritual health. The prayer our Lord taught us is full of wisdom along this line, "Give us this day our daily bread." That does not mean that if we do not pray we shall not get it. The word "give" has the sense of "receiving." When we become children of God we receive our daily bread from Him, the basis of blessing lies there, otherwise we take it as an animal with no discernment of God.

Possessions Outwitting Trust
Ecclesiastes 5:13-14

"There is a severe evil which I have seen under the sun: Riches kept for their owner to his hurt. But those riches perish through misfortune; when he begets a son, there is nothing in his hand."

If you have many possessions, it will ruin your trust and make you suspect everyone, and the better type of life is ruined. Again, you cannot hold your possessions, you may just overreach yourselves in possessions; or you may die and your children squander all you possessed. You cannot find lasting joy in these things, let them come and go, remain true to your relationship to God and don't put your trust in possessions. Live your life as a laborer, rightly related to mother earth, and to the providential order of tyranny; trust in God whatever happens, and the result will be that in your heart will be the joy that every man is seeking.

Personality, the Only Truth
Ecclesiastes 5:15-17

"As he came from his mother's womb, naked shall he return, to go as he came; and he take shall nothing from his labor which he may carry away in his hand. And this also is a severe evil, that just exactly as he came, so shall he go. And what profit has he who has labored for the wind? All his days he also eats in darkness, and he has much sorrow and sickness and anger."

Personal relationship brings us to the truth, and it is truth that relates one personally to God. Jesus said, "I am the truth." We have to form the mind of Christ, and it is not done at a leap. It is done by a maintained personal relationship to Jesus Christ, and slowly and surely the new mind is formed.

How many of us are working things out from the basis of a personal relationship to Jesus Christ? We work things out on the abstract logic of a sense of justice or of right. It is appalling to find spiritual people when they come into a crisis taking an ordinary common-sense standpoint as if Jesus Christ has never lived or died. It is a man's personal relationship that tells. When he dies he can take nothing he has done or made in his lifetime with him. The only thing he can take with him is what he *is*. There is no warrant in the Bible for the modern speculation of a second chance after death. Men may think there may be a second chance—but it is not taught in the Bible. The stage between birth and death is the probation stage.

We are apt to wrongly relate ourselves to books and to people. We often hear such remarks as—"The pastor is talking over the heads of the men;" or, "The Bible is all very well, but I don't understand it." It is never the thing you understand that does you good, but what is behind what is taught. If it is God's truth, you and I are going to meet it again whether we want to or not. The thing we value most in a meeting is not so much what is said, but the release that comes from the different atmosphere that is brought in, and we can begin to think. We benefit most by things over which we cannot be articulate, and if the truths we read or hear are the truths of God, they will crop up again. "A man's reach should exceed his grasp." The things we listen to and read ought to be beyond our comprehension, they go into our minds like seed thoughts, and slowly and surely bring forth fruit.

This is good counsel for boys and girls in their teens. We should always choose our books as God chooses our friends, just a bit beyond us, so that we have to do our level best to keep up with them. If we choose our own friends, we choose those we can lord it over.

Predominate Obligation in Time
Ecclesiastes 5:18-20

"Here is what I have seen: It is good and fitting for one to eat and drink, and to enjoy the good of all his labor in which he toils under the sun all the days of his life which

God gives him; for it is his heritage. As for every man to whom God has given riches and wealth, and given him power to eat of it, to receive his heritage and rejoice in his labor—this is the gift of God. For he will not dwell unduly on the days of his life, because God keeps him busy with the joy of his heart."

These verses are an astute summing up of a man's obligations in time. If a man becomes temporarily overwhelmed by anger or lust or false religion, the first thing that happens is that he will stop eating; no one can eat when he is in a rage. If you are in the habit of getting angry, you will soon get physically upset, the connection runs all through.

The test that a man is right with God is in eating and drinking. Solomon says, "It is good and fitting for one to eat and drink." Paul says, "Beware of those who teach abstinence from meats." . . . "Eat whatever is set before you, asking no question for conscience' sake." Remain true to God in your actual life. The right thing to do with riches is to enjoy your portion, and remember that what you lay by is a danger and a snare.

Solomon had everything a man could have in life, he had every means of satisfying himself; he tried the beastly line, the sublime line, the aesthetic line, the intellectual line; but, he says, you cannot find your lasting joy in any of them. Joy is only to be found in your relationship to God while you live on this earth, the earth you came from and the earth you return to. Dust is the finest element in man, because in it the glory of God is to be manifested.

The Bible makes much of a man's body. The teaching of Christianity on this point has been twisted by the influence of Plato's teaching, which says that a man can only further his moral and spiritual life by despising his body. The Bible teaches that the body is the temple of the Holy Spirit, it was molded by God of the dust of the ground and is man's chief glory, not his shame. When God became incarnate, "He took not on Him the nature of angels," but was made "in the likeness of men," and it is man's body that is yet to manifest the glory of God on earth. Material things are going to be translucent with the light of God.

Jesus Christ "came eating and drinking," and from Genesis to Revelation eating and drinking, and laboring in the ordinary toil of life in the condition of things as they are, are the things in which man will find his right relationship to life and to God.

The Edge of Things
Ecclesiastes 6:1-12

"When the Soul, growing clearer,
Sees God no nearer;
When the soul, mounting higher,
To God comes no nigher:
But the arch-fiend Pride,
Mounts at her side,
Foiling her high emprise,
Sealing her eagle eyes,
And, when she fain would soar,
Makes idols to adore—
Changing the pure emotion
Of her high devotion,
To a skin-deep sense
Of her own eloquence
Strong to deceive, strong to enslave—
Save. Oh! Save."

—Matthew Arnold

To say that the basis of things is not rational does not mean that a man does not have to be reasonable. A rationalist is not simply one who uses his reason, but one who says there is nothing at the basis of life that cannot be solved by ordinary reason and enlightenment. The question of tragedy, of the gap between mankind and God, on which the Bible bases everything, has nothing to do with the philosophy of a rationalist. To him sin is not a definite thing, it is a mere defect; consequently the need for redemption is emphatically ruled out. There is a tragedy and an agony at the basis of things that cannot be explained by reason; it must either be explained away, or faced in the way the Bible faces it. There is something wrong, and it can only be put right by redemption.

Many a man affects his doubts of God, they are purely intellectual. There is a phase when a man gets into tremendous stress of weather mentally, but there is also a phase when his doubts are a mere affectation. The Books of Wisdom are strong on facing facts, and yet there is no touch of despair underneath. In all other books which face things as they are, there is tremendous pessimism and abject despair, no hope whatever; but in Solomon's writings, while he maintains a ruggedness and an intensity and an unswerving truthfulness to facts, there is an extraordinary hopefulness running all through; and that without getting sentimental and falling back on the kindness of God. The minor prophets also state appalling facts—slaughters are crimes on foot are foretold enough to knock hope out of any one, but the Hebrew writers never seem to despair however bad the facts may be, there is always the indefinable certainty that there is something to hope about.

The Perils of Inevitable Barriers
Ecclesiastes 6:1-2

"There is an evil which I have seen under the sun, and it is common among men: A man to whom God has given riches and wealth and honor, so that he lacks nothing for himself of all he desires; yet God does not give him power to eat of it, but a foreigner consumes it. This is vanity, and it is an evil affliction."

A man may have all these things—riches, wealth, honor—and at the same time be the victim of an incurable disease. The Hebrew mind looks upon that as an act of God, something for which the man himself is not responsible. The question of the inevitable barriers comes out very strongly in the records of Bible characters. When the inevitable strikes, there is no whine, but rather an astonishing facing of the situation. These inevitable things are outside one's control, he is not asked about them, and when they enter as factors into his calculations they present him with a peril.

Suppose a man is very ambitious, and rightly so, then just as he has begun to attain his ambitions, he is alarmed over certain symptoms in himself and consults a doctor and the verdict of an incurable disease is passed. It is madness to think he will ever be able to fulfill his ambitions. The danger is that the man sink into crushing despair, while the courageous thing for him is to hand over to God what belongs to Him and to wait for His solution.

As one of the results of war, men have been ruined in thousands of cases so far as their future life on this planet is concerned. To look at facts as they are and to think them right out to the bottom makes a man a pessimist, not a despairer, but a pessimist. That means things are as bad as they can be; it is absurd to say they could be worse, it is impossible to conceive things worse. A hopeful attitude does not come by facing facts, or by not facing facts, but only by temperament or religion.

The inevitable barriers are there in every one of our

lives. They may not be of an intense order, such as a terrible maiming, or blindness, or deafness, or something that knocks a man out of fulfilling his ambitions, they may be hereditary incapabilities; but the peril is lest we lie down and whine and are no more good.

The thing to do is to recognize that the barriers are inscrutable, that they are there not by chance but entirely by God's permission, and they should be faced and not ignored. Was there ever a more severely handicapped life on this earth than Helen Keller's? The peril of the inevitable barriers is that if I have not faced the facts sufficiently, I am apt to blame God for them. There is one more fact that I do not know, and that fact lies entirely with God, not with me.

It is no use to spend my time saying, "I wish I was not like this." I am just like it. The practical point of Christianity is—Can Jesus Christ and His religion be of any use to me as I am, not as I am not? Can He deal with me where I am, in the condition I am in?

Preposterous and Inveterate Brutishness
Ecclesiastes 6:3

"If a man begets a hundred children and lives many years, so that the days of his years are many, but his soul is not satisfied with goodness, or indeed he has no burial, I say that a stillborn child is better than he."

In the Hebrew conception it was a disgrace for a man to have no burial (see 2 Ki. 9:34-35). This conception is remote from us today.

Solomon says: A man has no business to be an inveterate brute, to live to breed and eat and pile up goods without the slightest idea of the kind of monument his life is erecting—for himself he lives and for himself he dies. Solomon won't have the brute aspect of human life ignored; but to remember that I am a brute and to be brutish are two different things. It is a preposterous iniquity to be a brutish man, satisfied with being once-born (see Ps. 75:3-9).

The thing to do is to recognize that I am a brute, but I have the brute well under control. Solomon is talking of the man who will not recognize this. To ignore the fact that I am a man is the action of a fool, or of a mystic. To recognize it and see to it that I am a chaste man is the line the Bible insists on—Don't deny that you have a body, but insist on it that you can live in your body the kind of manhood that God demands. Solomon is speaking of the man who is a brute and brutish—"Yes, I am an animal, and I will glut my appetites as they come, I shall sink and not rise." Solomon says, "A stillborn child is better than he" (see Matt. 18:5).

There is a difference between doing wicked things and being a wicked person. When Jesus Christ saw the pariahs of His day, He did not say to them, "You are of your father the devil;" but He did say that to the Pharisees (see John 8:44). The Pharisees were play-actors, putting on what did not belong to them; but remember, too, that some of the best men in our Lord's day were Pharisees—Nicodemus, Saul of Tarsus. Jesus said to the Pharisees: "Tax collectors and harlots enter the kingdom of God before you." It was not the bad people who were guilty of the wicked things. We are apt to tone down the things our Lord tiraded against—pride, self-realization, etc. When a man is guilty of wrong things, he recognizes instantly that there is a chance of being delivered; but the righteous man sits self-governed in his own right, he is his own god.

Place of Invincible Banality
Ecclesiastes 6:4-8

"For it comes in vanity and departs in darkness, and its name is covered with darkness. Though it has not seen the sun or known anything this has more rest than that man, even if he lives a thousand years twice over but has not seen goodness. Do not all go to one place? All the labor of man is for his mouth, and yet the soul is not satisfied. For what more has the wise man than the fool? What does the poor man have who knows how to walk before the living?"

Solomon is referring to the man who lays up for himself and for others, and he does not commend him. Today we enthrone insurance and economy, but it is striking to recall that the one thing Jesus Christ commended was extravagance. Our Lord only called one work "good," and that was the act of Mary of Bethany when she broke the alabaster box of ointment. It was neither useful nor her duty, it sprang from her devotion to Jesus, and He said of it—"Wherever this gospel is preached in the whole world, what this woman has done will also be told as a memorial of her."

The object of a man's life is not to hoard; he has to get enough for his brute life and no more; the best of his life is to be spent in confidence in God. We are meant to utilize the earth and its products for food and the nourishment of our bodies, but we must not live in order to make our existence. If the children of Israel gathered more manna than they needed, it turned into dry rot, and that law still holds good.

When we learn this wisdom of the Hebrews we shall soon see how far away we are from it and from the teaching of Jesus Christ. Our Lord taught that a man ought to be carefully careless about everything except his relationship to

Himself. We who call ourselves Christians are tremendously far, almost opposingly far, from that central point of Christianity; it is not even intimate to us. Generation after generation of civilized life have been opposed to it, and as long as we are on the line of economy and insurance, Jesus Christ cannot have His innings.

In personal life, in church life, and in national life, we try Jesus Christ's teaching, but as soon as it becomes difficult we abandon it, or else we compromise. "Therefore do not worry, saying, What shall we eat? or, What shall we drink? or What shall we wear?" Bank your faith in God, do the duty that lies nearest and "damn the consequences." Who is prepared to do this, prepared to stake his all on Jesus Christ and His Word? We do it in preaching and in books, but not in practical life. We put our emphasis on the other line, trusting in our wits, and God is left out of it. When once we are related to Jesus Christ, our relation to actual life is that of a child, perfectly simple and marvelous.

Perdition of Individual Burning
Ecclesiastes 6:9

"Better is the sight of the eyes than the wandering of desire."

Lust applies not only to the bestial side of things; lust means literally—"I must have it at once, and I don't care what the consequences are." It may be a low, animal lust, or it may be a mental lust, or a moral or spiritual lust; but it is a characteristic that does not belong to the life hid with Christ in God. Love is the opposite; love can wait endlessly.

"Better is the sight of the eyes, than the wandering of

desire." One of the first things Jesus Christ does is to open a man's eyes and he sees things as they are. Until then he is not satisfied with the seeing of his eyes, he wants more, anything that is hidden he must drag to the light, and the wandering of desire is the burning waste of a man's life until he finds God. His heart lusts, his mind lusts, his eyes lust, everything in him lusts until he is related to God. It is the demand for an infinite satisfaction and it ends in the perdition of a man's life.

Jesus Christ says, "Come to Me, and I will give you rest"—I will put you in the place where your eyes are open. And notice what Jesus Christ says we will look at—lilies, and sparrows, and grass. What man in his senses bothers about these things! We consider airplanes and tanks and shells because these demand our attention, the other things do not. The great emancipation in the salvation of God is that it gives a man the sight of his eyes, and he sees for the first time the handiwork of God in a daisy. No longer has he a burning lust that turns everything into a howling wilderness of wrong.

"But their eyes were restrained, so that they did not know him." "Then their eyes were opened and they knew Him" (Luke 24:16, 31). We see our friend, the other man sees a fellow in a shirt, we *perceive* the man inside the shirt. When Jesus Christ asked His disciples "Who do men say that I, the Son of Man, am?" He was referring to this perception. To the majority of men Jesus Christ was only a Nazarene carpenter, but He says—"Who do *you* say that I am?" "Even though we have known Christ according to the flesh, yet now we know Him thus no longer" (2 Cor. 5:16). The salvation of Jesus Christ enables a man to see for the first time in his life, and it is a wonderful thing.

"Heaven above is brighter blue.
   Earth around is sweeter green,
Something lives in every hue
   Christless eyes have never seen;
Birds with gladder songs o'erflow
   Flowers with deeper beauties shine,
Since I know, as now I know,
   I am His and He is mine."

Predisposition by Inspired Beginnings
Ecclesiastes 6:10-12

"Whatever one is, he has been named already, for it is
known that he is man; and he cannot contend with Him
who is mightier than he. Since there are many things that
increase vanity, how is man the better? For who knows
what is good for man in life, all the days of his vain life
which he passes like a shadow? Who can tell a man what
will happen after him under the sun?"

The Hebrew books of wisdom are all of a piece with the
first three chapters of Genesis. In order to estimate man
properly in the "soup" he is in just now, we must remember
what he was in the beginning. God created man in His own
image, a son of God. Adam and Eve were to have control
over the life in the air and on the earth and in the sea, on
one condition—that they allowed God to rule them absolutely. Man was to develop the earth and his own life until
he was transfigured. But instead there came the introduction
of sin, man took the rule over himself, he became his own
god, and thereby lost control over everything else. It is this
that accounts for the condition of things as they are now.

If we are going to have a sympathetic understanding of
the Bible, we must rid ourselves of the abominable conceit

that we are the wisest people that have ever been on the earth; we must stop our patronage of Jesus Christ and of the Bible, and have a bigger respect for the fundamental conception of life as it is. At the basis of Hebrew wisdom first of all, is confidence in God; and second, a terrific sigh and sob over the human race as a magnificent ruin of what God designed it to be. Modern wisdom says that man is a magnificent promise of what he is going to be. If that point of view is right, then there is no need to talk about sin and redemption, and the Bible is a cunningly devised fable. But the Bible point of view seems to cover most of the facts.

What Price This?
Ecclesiastes 7:1-7

"Indeed the Idols I have loved so long
Have done my credit in Men's Eye much wrong:
　　Have drown'd my Honor in a shallow Cup
And sold my reputation for a Song.

Indeed, indeed, Repentance oft before
I swore—but was I sober when I swore?
　　And then and then came Spring and Rose-in-hand
My thread-bare Penitence a-pieces tore." —Omar Khayyam

What a man prizes highly, he prices and praises accordingly.
Everything has its price and can be bought. Men and women
can be bought. We are bought on the low level of swine, or
bribery, or moral compromise, or spiritual insurance; and we
are bought with the precious blood of Christ.

　　Solomon rattles the bottom board out of every piece of
deception. The only true joy in life, he says, is based on a
personal relationship to God. You cannot find joy in being
like animals, or in art, or aestheticism, in ruling or being
ruled—the whole thing is passed in survey in a most ruth-
less examination by a man whose wisdom is profounder than

93

the profoundest and has never been excelled, and in summing it all up he says that joy is only found in any of these things when a man is rightly related to God.

An elemental thing to remember is that we must never read into a man's words what we mean, but must try and find out what the author of the words means. As a rule we read into his words what we mean and consequently miss his meaning altogether. Before we can criticize a man's statements we must find out his meaning, find out what kind of a genius or fool he was who said it. If we do this with the Bible, it will put the statements made there in quite another light. If the man on the street (for example, just you and me) is going to prove the truth of Christianity, he must "come off the street owning its power." If we do not intend to go out of our own ways of looking at things, we shall never find out the other man's ways of looking at them.

The Attainment of Sagacious Character
Ecclesiastes 7:1

"A good name is better than precious ointment, and the day of death than the day of one's birth."

Solomon is speaking of character, not of reputation. Reputation is what other people think of you; "character is what you are in the dark," where no one sees but yourself. That is where the worth of a man's character lies, and Solomon says that the man who has attained a sagacious character during life is like a most refreshing, soothing, healing ointment. In the New Testament, *name* frequently has the meaning of "nature." "Where two or three are gathered together in My name"—My nature (Matt. 18:20). Everyone who comes across a good nature is made better by it, unless he is determined to be bad.

To say that someone has a good nature does not mean he is a pious individual, always quoting texts. The test of a nature is the atmosphere it produces. When we are in contact with a good nature we are uplifted by it. We do not get anything we can state articulately, but the horizon is enlarged, the pressure is removed from the mind and heart and we see things differently.

The Advantage of a Sad Condition
Ecclesiastes 7:2

"It is better to go to the house of mourning than to go to the house of feasting, for that is the end of all men; and the living will take it to heart."

Solomon is not implying that it is better to grouse around in the luxury of misery than to feast; he is dealing with finding true essential joy, and he says if ever we are going to have a true estimate of life we shall have to face it at its worst. All through the books of Hebrew wisdom there is this certainty that the basis of actual life is tragedy. Human nature is a ruin of what it once was, and a man is a fool to ignore that. If you want to know the basis of life, it is better to go to the house of mourning than to the house of pleasure. Remember, there is death, and there is worse than death—sin and tragedy and the possibility of terrible evil.

Solomon does not mean we should live as some folks who seem never to be happy unless they are at a funeral. He means us to keep at the basis of things, to scrape through the veneer and face things, and we learn to do this better in mourning than in feasting. "Do not appear to men to be fasting." If you have had a sad dose, don't pull a long face. Cover it up, don't let anyone imagine you are going through what you are.

If a man builds his life over a volcano, one day there will come terrific havoc. If we ignore the safety valves in mother earth, we will have to pay the penalty. Mount Vesuvius is one of the pumps that keeps the earth in proper order; the Creator has put His danger signals there, and yet people ignore them and plant their vineyards on its slopes, then when an eruption occurs we blame God and say how cruel He is to allow it.

No wise man will build up his life without knowing what the basis of life is, and Solomon indicates that a man can only arrive at a true view of life by brooding on the underlying tragedy.

The Appropriateness of Sorrow and Chastisement
Ecclesiastes 7:3

"Sorrow is better than laughter, for by a sad countenance the heart is made better."

"Countenance" means more than the face; the countenance is the whole aspect of one's nature (see Ps. 37:5, 11). To say "I won't countenance it" does not mean to show disapproval in my face, but that I refuse to give the thing the approval of my personal life. The man who has faced the fact that the basis of life is tragic is the one who begins to see the true relation of things, and he says, "I will go softly all my years."

We may find that the man who is remarkably cheerful now has gone through a hell that would make us shudder to face. The men and women who have been through things have always plenty of leisure for others, they never obtrude their own experiences. Many a man has found God in the belly of hell during war. He has come face to face with God through having had things stripped off and having to face the fact that the basis of life is tragedy.

The Aspects of Shallowness and Censure
Ecclesiastes 7:4-5

"The heart of the wise is in the house of mourning. But the heart of fools is in the house of mirth. It is better to hear the rebuke of the wise than for a man to hear the song of fools."

Solomon says that the house of mourning is the place where a man learns wisdom, he won't be so sharp with his tongue. There are things he might have said but he won't. No one who faces the ultimate tragedy in another's life can be the cheap and easy cynic we are all apt to be without thinking. Whistler wrote a book entitled *The Gentle Art of Making Enemies*—a miserably spiteful thing to do!

Go to the house of mourning and see your friend dead, and it will alter your attitude to things; don't be shallow. There is a place for the shallow, however, as well as the profound. One of the greatest defects in Christianity is that it is not shallow enough, in this respect it knows a great deal better than Jesus Christ. It is religious enough, supernormally moral, but not able to eat, drink, and be merry. Jesus Christ made the shallow and the profound, the give and the take, one. The art of shallow conversation is one that is rarely learned. It is a great gift as well as a real ministration to be able to say *nothing* cleverly. It is an insult to be everlastingly introducing subjects that make people think on the deepest lines. It takes all the essence of Christianity to be shallow properly.

The shallowness Solomon mentions here is that of refusing to realize that there is a basis of tragedy. A man who tells his chum with a broken heart to go to a cinema show is a fool. He ought to know that the house of shallowness is not the place for him, but that Jesus Christ is the only One who can heal him. It is a question of having a wise heart through facing the reality of things. When a man has "the heart of the wise," he is able to counsel his friend in the dark way.

The Atrophy of Sagacity by Clownishness
Ecclesiastes 7:6

"For like the crackling of thorns under a pot, so is the laughter of the fool. This also is vanity."

The private history of a professional clown may be one of the saddest. The man who sets himself to make others laugh has often an immensely sad life of his own behind. He can kill his own wisdom by living apart; he can atrophy his real life by keeping up a certain role. If a man has a name for being smart, he may find it a job to keep up the role. When you take up the clownish line, you kill something that ought not to be killed. You atrophy the wisest part of your nature. It takes a tremendous amount of relationship to God for a man to *be* what he is.

The Anachronism of Conscientiousness
Ecclesiastes 7:7

"Surely oppression destroys a wise man's reason, and a bribe debases the heart."

Anachronism means anything out of keeping with the time. A wise person who has built his life in confidence in God will appear a fool when he is among people who are sleek and cunning. "Extortion" makes the wisdom of the wisest appear fools. You can ridicule anyone, even Jesus Christ. The wisdom of God is arrant stupidity to the wisdom of the world, until all of a sudden God makes the wisdom of the world foolish (see 1 Cor. 1:23-25).

If you stand true to your faith in God, there will be situations in which you will come across extortioners, cunning, crafty people, who use their wits instead of worshiping God, and you will appear a fool. Are you prepared to appear a fool for Christ's sake? Very few of us know anything about suffering for Christ's sake for conscience or conviction's sake. To suffer for Christ's sake is to suffer because of being personally related to Him.

If you are going to be true to God, you will appear a fool among those who do not believe in God, and you must lay your account with this. Jesus said, "Therefore whoever confesses ME before men . . . " and it tests a man for all he is worth to confess Jesus Christ, because the confession has to be made in the set he belongs to and esteems. The "shame" of the gospel. "I am not ashamed of the gospel of Christ," says Paul.

No man can confess Jesus Christ without realizing the cost to others; if he states this, he rebukes them. The Spirit of God may lay hold of one man among a crowd of men to be related to God, but his sense of honor may keep him from going through—I don't want to appear different from the others; if I go through with this and relate myself to Jesus Christ, I shall be a speckled bird and look superior.

Many a man is kept from coming to Jesus because his own crowd is not going that road. It is a standard of honor, but a standard of honor not rightly related. In the life of a disciple it is the honor of Jesus Christ that is at stake, not our own honor. Your crowd matters to you, but your crowd does not matter to me; nor do you need to care what my crowd thinks of you. But take a step aside from your own immediate circle, and you will have to reckon with what they say about you (see Heb. 13:13).

In Christian experience what stands in the way of my obedience to God is not the cost to me, but the cost to my father and mother and others. "If any one comes to Me, and does not hate his father, and mother . . . he cannot be my disciple." Jesus Christ's penetration comes straight home. Think what it cost Jesus Christ's mother and His friends for Him to be true to God. If He had not been true to what He came to do, His mother would not have had the sword pierce her heart; His own nation would not have blasphemed the Holy Spirit. In going on with God this is where we find the anachronism comes in—according to the astute wisdom of the world we live in, we are made to do or say the thing at the wrong time.

This is brought home by tragedies such as war. It is not a question of what it costs the individual men to join up, but of the cost to those who belong to them; the strain the wives and mothers and fathers and children have to bear. That is the terrific cost to the man who goes out to fight his country's battles. No man can tell why he enlisted. The watchword "For Monarch and Country" is too shallow. The sacrifice he makes is never intended for man, it is meant for God, and is to be poured out before the Lord, as David poured out the water from the well of Bethlehem (see 2 Sam. 23:14-17).

Something Doing
Ecclesiastes 7:8-12

"And is it that the haze of grief
Makes former gladness loom so great?
The lowness of the present state,
That sets the past in this relief?

Or that the past will always win
A glory from its being far,
An orb into the perfect star
We saw not, when we moved therein."

—Tennyson

There is a tendency in us all to mourn over something—to say that the past was a great deal better than the present, or that the future will be better; the worst time we ever lived in is the present—forgetting that we never lived in any other time!

Because a thing is good enough for us, or for an age, or for a nation, is not sufficient to make it the truth. It may be a statement that will do for a time, but unless we have been dumped down onto the basis of things, our experience is of no avail as a revelation of the foundation of life. It is the extraordinary thinker, the man with the extreme experience, rather than the average individual, who gets at the truth at the basis of things. When we deal with great thinkers like Solomon or Shakespeare we get to the truth of things; we do not get the truth through experience. Most of us do not *think*; we live healthy ordinary lives and don't bother about thinking at all. But when an upheaval comes from underneath proving that the basis of things is not rational, we find the value of the Bible attitude, which is that the basis of things is tragic and not rational. We have to live based on our relationship to God in the actual condition of things as they are.

The End Explains—
And the Patient Excels the Proud
Ecclesiastes 7:8

"The end of a thing is better than its beginning, and the patient in spirit is better than the proud in spirit."

"The end explains," not "The end justifies the means"—that is never right. If you live as an animal, the end will explain that you have made a mess of things. If you live morally, the end will explain that you have lived morally. "End" has the meaning of "issue" (see Jer. 29:11 RSV, marg.). When death ends the present order, the issue will reveal how you have lived. Only when you live in personal relationship to God does the end explain that you have the right secret of life.

In the book of Revelation (which is the Apocalypse of the New Testament as the Song of Solomon is the Apocalypse of the Old Testament), Jesus Christ refers to Himself as "the first and the last." It is in the middle that human choices are made; the beginning and the end remain with God. The decrees of God are birth and death, and in between those limits man makes his own distress or joy.

Solomon counsels us not to be staggered when we find oppressors and tyrants around, the end will explain all. It is not enough to say that because my religious beliefs do for me, therefore they are satisfactory. If everyone were well brought up and had a good heredity, any number of intellectual forms of belief would do. The test of a man's religion is not what it does for him, but what it does for the worst man he knows.

The Excitement of Exasperation— And Discretion Excels Domineering
Ecclesiastes 7:9

"Do not hasten in your spirit to be angry, for anger rests in the bosom of fools."

All through the Bible, emphasis is laid steadily on patience. A man's patience is tested by three things—God, himself, and other people. An apt illustration is that of a bow and arrow in the hand of an archer. God is not aiming at what we are, nor is He asking our permission. He has us in His hands for His own purpose, and He strains to the last limit; then when He lets fly, the arrow goes straight to His goal. "Acquire your soul with patience." Don't get impatient with yourself.

The Bible is a relation of facts, the truth of which must be tested. Life may go on all right for a while, when suddenly a bereavement comes, or some crisis; unrequited love or a new love, a disaster, a business collapse, or a shocking sin, and we turn to our Bibles again and God's Word comes straight home. And we say, "Why, I never saw that there before." As long as you live a logical life without realizing the deeper depths of your personality, the Bible does not amount to anything; but strike lower down where mathematics and logic are of no account, and you find that Jesus Christ and the Bible tell every time.

Truth is never a matter of intellect first, but of moral obedience. The great secret of intellectual progress is curiosity, but curiosity in moral matters is an abomination. Moral sophistry says—Go and find out for yourself. If I do, I am a fool. I don't care what a man's moral strength is, I defy him to start on the line of moral curiosity without instantly damning some of the finer sensibilities of his life. "But of the tree of the knowledge of good and evil you shall not eat, for in the day that you eat of it you shall surely die" (Gen. 2:17). We are not to know evil by eating of the fruit of the tree; if we do eat of the tree we shall die. If you are pitchforked into moral filth, you will be kept; but if you go into it from curiosity you will not be kept, no one goes into it without coming out soiled. You may be physically clean, but you have lost something.

The essential element in moral life is obedience and submission. If you want spiritual truth, obey the highest standard you know. "If anyone wants to do His will, he shall know concerning the doctrine, whether it is from God or whether I speak on My own authority" (John 7:17). Intellectually, curiosity is the thing; morally, obedience is what is needed. One *ounce* of chastity is worth fifty years of intellect in moral discernment. Moral truth is never reached by intellect, but only through conscience. When a fine keen intellect and moral obedience go together, we find the mind that is beginning to discover step by step where goodness and truth lie.

"Anger rests in the bosom of fools." Solomon's warning is that a man who excites himself to exasperation is a fool, because simulated indignation produces the thing itself. For instance, if in the morning you begin to snarl, in less than half an hour you will feel thoroughly bad tempered. The man who can curb his spirit and control himself is wise, and is better than one who can take a city.

Discretion excels domineering. Obstinacy and strength of will are often confounded, but they are very different. An obstinate man is unintelligent; a strong-minded man is one who has made up his mind on a matter but is prepared to listen to your arguments and deal with them, and show to your satisfaction that his decision is right. A stubborn man is always a "small potato."

We may make up our minds easily, but to make up a mind of any breadth takes time, there are so many sides to every matter. If you have made up your mind on the line of strength and not of obstinacy, when you are questioned you don't domineer. Domineering is the intellectual side of stubbornness, and is a sign of moral weakness. It is absurd to mistake the expression of physical stubbornness, such as a square jaw, for strength of will; tenacity of will may go with a jaw like a child's top. Will is not a thing I possess; will is the whole person active. Solomon is pointing out that the man who is excited into exasperation is weak, a fool, and if he begins to domineer it shows he has no discretion. There are some things that can be answered straight off and others that cannot.

"Do not hasten in your spirit to be angry." Anger nearly always covers up a thing that is wrong. Suppose you have been in the wrong in a certain matter and no one knows it but yourself, and then you are wrongfully accused of something else, you are so thankful that the real thing was not discovered that you make protestations of innocence as if you were spotlessly right all through. It is an indication that there is weakness and foolishness somewhere. Never domineer, and never get exasperated unless you want to be a fool.

The Religion of Reminiscence—
and the Present Excels the Past
Ecclesiastes 7:10

"Do not say, 'Why were the former days better than these?' For you do not inquire wisely concerning this."

At the beginning of the war, what was called the Christian religion was mainly a cult of reminiscence. Take any denomination you like, and the religious bodies that do not consider themselves denominations—was their main object the establishment of a family likeness to Jesus Christ? No, their main object was to establish the particular creed they upheld, consequently when the crisis struck us, the religious element of the country was powerless to grip the situation. Individual spiritual people were not powerless; in every denomination there were those who were the true salt of earth, but the external phase of religion was not able to grapple with the situation. The passion of reminiscence was ruling everywhere, the old ways of doing things.

A revival adds nothing, it simply brings back what had been lost and is a confession of failure. The effects of a revival may be deplorable. "Oh that we had the ancient days of simplicity and sunshine"—days of adversity and humbug! Things are bad and difficult now, but not a tithe as difficult as they used to be. It is of no use to pray for the old days; stand square where you are and make the present better than any past has been. Base all on your relationship to God and go forward, and presently you will find that what is emerging is infinitely better than the past ever was. The present excels the past because we have the wealth of the past to go on. Solomon is not talking evolution, but simple fact.

The Wisdom of the World
and the World of Wisdom
Ecclesiastes 7:11-12

"Wisdom is good with an inheritance, and profitable to those who see the sun. For wisdom is a defense as money is a defense, but the excellence of knowledge is that wisdom gives life to those who have it."

Solomon says that that compromise will deceive you. If a man is honest because it pays him to be, he ceases to be honest. "You cannot serve God and mammon." We say we can because we do not see God. If I only see you, I will wink the other eye—you trick me and I'll trick you. Civilization is based on murder, it is wisdom with an inheritance, keep the two things going. As long as you try the juggling trick you will find the teaching of Jesus Christ is nonsense, but any man who dares to take God at His Word will find it works every time.

The world of wisdom is to bank all on God and disregard the consequences. People are told to "decide for Christ"; no one can do it; what one has to do is deliberately commit himself to Jesus Christ. We get hold of the size of our dastardly impertinence when we say to God—"No, I can't trust Your word; I can't live the kind of life You require." Are we prepared to stake our all on the honor of Jesus Christ? Immediately a man is driven to distress and he realizes that he must sink anyhow, he goes straight to Jesus Christ and finds that instead of sinking, he is lifted up and receives salvation. Stake everything on the honor of Jesus Christ, and you will find you have struck bedrock. Whenever our spiritual life is unsatisfactory it is because we have said to God—"I won't"; You can't expect me to trust You." Then we must take the consequences. "And He did not do many mighty works there because of their unbelief." If Jesus Christ has done no mighty works for me it is either because I don't believe He can, or I don't want Him to. I may say—"Oh yes, I believe Jesus Christ will give me the Holy Spirit"; but I am not prepared for Him to do it, I don't want Him to. Will you launch out on what Jesus says? If you will, you will find that God is as good as His Word.

Get to the place where you make the thing inevitable, burn your bridges behind you, make retreat impossible, then go ahead. Solomon's counsel is wise—"Trust in the Lord with all your heart; and lean not on your own understanding." It is leaning to our own understanding that keeps the bridges behind.

"Over the Top"
Ecclesiastes 7:13-22

When the time comes to act, it has to be a going over the top—over the top of everything you have been entrenched in—prejudices, beliefs—all.

Inevitable and Attainable
Ecclesiastes 7:13

"Consider the work of God; for who can make straight what He has made crooked?"

All the Hebrew prophets and the New Testament apostles make a distinction between the inevitable and the attainable. There are inevitable things for which a man is not responsible. For instance, I cannot say when I will be born or when I will die; birth and death are inevitable. I have to attain within the two on the basis of things as they are. If this distinction between the inevitable and the attainable is not made, it will lead to a muddle in the presentation of evangelical religion.

When a man goes "over the top," he sees things as he never saw them before. He comes across things he cannot diagnose or understand, and he begins to flounder and wonders what he ought to do. The thing for him to do is to base on the inevitable and then find out what is attainable.

No man can redeem his own soul, or give himself a new heredity; that is the work of the sovereign grace of God. Man has nothing to do with redemption, it is God's "bit"; but God cannot give a man a good character, that is not God's business, nor is it an inevitable thing. God will give us what we cannot give ourselves, a totally new heredity (see Luke 12:13). God will put the disposition of His Son, the Holy Spirit, into any man who asks, then on that basis man has to work out a holy character. "*Work out* your own salvation with fear and trembling; for it is God who *works in* you."

"Who can make straight what He has made crooked?" In our talks on the Book of Job we mentioned the refraction of God in the universe.[1] What man finds it easy to explain actual facts as he sees them today in connection with his belief in God? Job is the expression of a man who suffered in this way. In theory God appears to be just and kind, but in actual life things seem to flatly contradict His justice and kindness. It is part of common sense to be atheistic rather than to believe in the refraction of God in the universe. Solomon says that if we try and work things out on the line of intellect, on a theory of goodness or justice, we will always find the refraction. There is something wrong at the basis of things, and it cannot be put right until another inevitable thing happens—

---

[1] "Whenever God presents Himself in the present order of the material universe, He appears to go crooked, that is, crooked to our reason; we cannot understand Him. God allows things in the cosmic world which are a refraction: they do not continue in the straight simple line my mind tells me they ought to take .... If you try to weave a conception of God out of Jesus Christ's presentation of Him and then look at life as it is, you will find what is meant by the cosmic refraction of God—the God revealed in Jesus Christ is flatly contradicted in the natural world" (see Rom. 8:20-22). (*Baffled to Fight Better* pp. 56-57.)

the manifestation of the children of God. The thing to do is to place our faith in God and attain morally in the midst of things, crooked as they appear. Watch the inevitable things, and don't try to work out the riddle of the universe.

Instructive and Aggregate
Ecclesiastes 7:14

"In the day of prosperity be joyful, but in the day of adversity consider: Surely God has appointed the one as well as the other, so that man can find nothing that will happen after him."

The test of elemental honesty is the way a man behaves himself in grief and in joy. The natural elemental man expresses his joy or sorrow straight off. Today in our schools boys are taught stoicism; it produces an admirable type of lad externally, but not so admirable internally. When we are rightly related to God we must let things have their way with us and not pretend things are not as they are. It is difficult not to simulate sorrow or gladness but to remain natural and steadfastly true to God as things come. Don't deal only with the section that is sad or with the section that is joyful, deal with them together. When we accept God's purpose for us in Christ Jesus, we know that *all things work together for good.*

Stoicism has the effect of making a man hysterical and sentimental, it produces a denseness spiritually. When you are joyful, be joyful; when you are sad, be sad. If God has given you a sweet cup, don't make it bitter; and if He has given you a bitter cup, don't try and make it sweet; take things as they come. One of the last lessons we learn is not to be an amateur providence—"I shall not allow that person to suffer." Suffering, and the inevitable result of suffering, is the only way some of us can learn, and if we are shielded God will ultimately take the one who interferes by the scruff of the neck and remove him. The fingers that caress a child may also hurt its flesh; it is the power of love that makes them hurt.

Irreparable and Anticlimax
Ecclesiastes 7:15

"I have seen all things in my days of vanity: There is a just man who perishes in his righteousness, and there is a wicked man who prolongs his life in his wickedness."

For a man to have doubts is not a sign that he is a bad man. David was up against things in his day—"Surely I have cleansed my heart in vain, and washed my hands in innocence. For all the day long I have been plagued, and chastened every morning" (Ps. 73:13-14).

Sum up the life of Jesus Christ by any other standard than God's, and it is an anticlimax of failure. "It is required in stewards that one be found faithful"—not successful. The anticlimax comes when we look for rewards—"If I am good, I shall be blessed." The logic of mathematics does not amount to anything in the spiritual realm. If a man has had a good beginning of splendid uprightness, and all the advantages of a good education, we may say he is sure to attain. There never was a sunnier beginning than Samson's, and yet he ended in a frantic collapse. There are irreparable things and anticlimaxes in life, and the explanation is not to be found on the rational line, but on the line of personal relationship to God. Remain true to God, and remember that certain things are irreparable. There is no road back to yesterday, it is only God on the basis of redemption who can get back to yesterday. Logic and reason have to do with things based on space and time, but they cannot push beyond space and time. We are all agnostic about God, about the Spirit of God, and prayer. It is nonsense to call prayer reasonable; it is the most super-reasonable thing there is.

The war has produced anticlimaxes in hundreds of lives, men are maimed and useless for fulfilling their ambitions. You rarely hear a man who has been through the real agony of suffering say that he disbelieves in God; it is the one who watches others going through suffering who says he disbelieves in God. In the suffering there is a compensation which cannot be got at in any other way. It is not seen from the outside because the compensation cannot be stated articulately.

Introspective and Abnormal
Ecclesiastes 7:16

"Do not be overly righteous, nor be overly wise; why should you destroy yourself?"

Solomon is dealing with the fact that a man ought not to be either a religious fanatic or a stupid fool. Don't be fanatical, he says, remember you have an actual life to live. A fanatic sees God's order but remains invincibly ignorant about God's permissive will. The spiritual fanatic ignores the actual life and says—"Jesus Christ said there is no marrying and giving in marriage in heaven, so there must be none on earth." That is being overwise.

If you examine yourself too much, you unfit yourself for life. There is a stage in life when introspection is necessary, but if it is pushed too far you become abnormally hypersensitive, either in conceit or grovelling. Introspection is the result of love or of anything elemental. When a man falls in love, he feels he is not worthy to crawl on the earth by the side of his divinity! The same thing spiritually; when once a man sees God he is apt to forget that he has to live on this planet. Solomon's counsel is to live an earthly life on the basis of things as they are, and not to compromise or be overwise.

It is easier to cut ourselves off from actual things and to nourish a life of our own intellectually. An intellectual man sums up other men by their brains, as Carlyle did, and he is apt to become contemptuous. A man is more than his brain. A man who lives a mystical life or an intellectual life frequently has an attitude of lofty contempt towards others. No one has any right to maintain such an attitude towards another human being, watching him as a spectator for purposes of his own, as journalistic copy, or as a religious specimen; if he does he ceases to be a human being by pretending to be more.

Iniquitous and Anarchic
Ecclesiastes 7:17

"Do not be overly wicked, nor be foolish: why should you die before your time."

Don't go to the opposite extreme and say, "I am going to live as I choose. The right attitude is between the two—neither "overwise" nor "over much wicked."

In the incarnation we see the right amalgam—pure deity and the pure human mixed. The talk about pure Deity is an intellectual conceit, it sounds winning to aesthetic culture, but it has no worth in a man's practical life. An almighty, incomprehensible, incognoscible being does not amount to anything to me. It is when God becomes incarnate that we see the right amalgam, dust and deity made one, human flesh presenced with divinity. That is the meaning of the incarnation, and Jesus Christ claims He can do it for any one of us. Man cannot be pure deity and he cannot be pure dust; he has to have the right alloy—dust and deity, made one by drudgery, and this produces the type of life with the right balance.

Injunction and Anathema
Ecclesiastes 7:18

"It is good that you grasp this, and also not remove your hand from the other; for he who fears God will escape them all."

Don't be fanatically religious and don't be irreverently blatant. Remember that the two extremes have to be held in the right balance. If your religion does not make you a better man, it is a rotten religion. The test of true religion is when it touches these four things—food, money, sex, and mother earth. These things are the test of a right, sane life with God, and the religion that ignores them or abuses them is not right. God made man of the dust of the ground, and that dust can express either deity or devilishness.

Remember we are not to be numbskulls, but holy men, full-blooded and holy to the last degree, not anemic creatures without enough strength to be bad. The relation to life ordained by Jesus Christ does not unsex men and women, but enables them to be holy men and women. "The love of money is a root of all kinds of evil" (1 Tim. 6:10). Money is a test, another thing which proves a man's religion; and the way a man treats the soil will also prove whether or not he is a son of God. A man needs to hold a right attitude to all these things by means of his personal relationship to God.

Intelligent and Animal
Ecclesiastes 7:19

"Wisdom strengthens the wise more than ten rulers of the city."

"He who rules his spirit [is better] than he who takes a city" (Prov. 16:32). An intelligent man in a city, one who is guided by sagacity, is worth ten strong men who guard the city. It is the mobilization of invention that is telling more and more. The man who is able to make use of sagacious inventions is worth a dozen people with mere strength, because he makes use of the strength of others. Our great commanders and leaders have not always been strong men physically. It is not always true that a sound mind is in a sound body; the finest of minds are often in impaired bodies, and some of the most sordid minds in healthy bodies.

Impeccable and Artificial
Ecclesiastes 7:20

"For there is not a just man on earth who does good and does not sin."

Impeccable—liable not to sin. The idea that because Jesus Christ was without sin therefore He could not be tempted, has become woven into religious belief. If that were so, the record of His temptation is a mere farce. Could Jesus Christ be tempted? Undoubtedly He could, because temptation and sin are not the same thing. "In all points tempted . . . . yet without sin." No good man is impeccable, that is, he never arrives at the place where it is impossible to sin. A man is able not to sin, but it never becomes impossible to sin. "Whoever has been born of God does not sin; for

His seed remains in him; and he cannot sin, because he has been born of God" (1 John 3:9). The life of God is born in us, and the life of God cannot sin; that does not mean that we *cannot* sin; but that if we obey the life of God in us, we *need not* sin.

The best of men are but the best of men. Don't glory in men; don't say, I am of Paul; I am of Apollos. Bank your confidence in God, not in men. Unless we are damnable, we are not worth saving. If we cannot go to the devil, we cannot go to God. The measure of the depth to which a man can fall is the height to which he can rise. Virtue is the outcome of conflict not of necessity.

Invidious and Argumentative
Ecclesiastes 7:21-22

"Also do not take to heart everything people say, lest you hear your servant cursing you. For many times, also, your own heart has known that even you have cursed others."

This is an inexorable law. "I am perfectly certain So-and-so has been criticizing me." Well, what have you been saying about him? Watch the process. It is as certain as God's throne, the measure you mete will be meted to you, not necessarily by the same person. Tit for tat is the inevitable law in actual life. Don't talk too much, says Solomon; if you talk too much, others will too. Don't be a busybody in other men's matters. A gossip is not always the bad person he is made out to be, those who listen and don't talk are the dangerous folk. The scandalmonger gets the blame, but the others are worse. A lie is not simply "a terminological inexactitude;" a lie is a truth told with bad intent. I may repeat the exact words of someone else and yet tell a lie because I convey a wrong meaning. Be careful, says Solomon, not to talk too much, because what you say will be taken up by others.

In the Sty
Ecclesiastes 7:23-29

"O me, why have they not buried me deep enough?
Is it kind to have made me a grave so rough,
Me, that was never a quiet sleeper?
Maybe still I am but half dead;
Then I cannot be wholly dumb;
I will cry to the steps above my head
And somebody, surely, some kind heart will come
To bury me, bury me
Deeper, ever so little deeper."

—Tennyson

The Bible deals with the worst tragedy that human nature and the devil could concoct. We seem to have forgotten this nowadays. The atonement has been made a kind of moral "lavatory" wherein a man can wash and go out and get dirty again. But when a man like Solomon or Shakespeare or Ibsen lifts the veil from the basis of things (which most of us know nothing of because we are too dense or too remote from it), we find that the redemption deals with tragedy of an appalling order.

When the war broke out, the ruling note in religion was

being struck not by the men and women who knew the basis of things, but by those who were unfamiliar with the abominable tragedy at the basis of human life, such as is being exhibited now; consequently something feeble and ethereal and totally unlike the Bible was ruling, and being expressed in unrobust prayer meetings and in hymns and poems by anemic people of both sexes. Our religious life was built up by people who were not dealing with tragedy. When civilized life is burst into we find what Solomon indicates, that the basis of life is tragic. No education, no culture, no sociology or government can touch the fathomless rot at the basis of human life in its deepest down story. We live in the twenty-second story up, and the tragedies we touch are only personal tragedies; only one in a million comes to understand the havoc that underlies everything. This line of thinking is absolutely important, not relatively important.

Program and Plague of the Heart
Ecclesiastes 7:23-24

"All this I have proved by wisdom. I said, 'I will be wise'; but it was far from me. As for that which is far off and exceedingly deep, who can find it out?"

Solomon deliberately set himself to find out things and to live according to the highest possible wisdom, but, he says, "it was far from me." He discovered what every lad who has been well brought up and has had a decent amount of natural religion in his life experiences, when he finds that his ideals cannot be realized. A young person sees more clearly, dreams more purely and has higher thoughts in his teens than ever he does afterwards. Then he goes through the severest of struggles—I cannot bring my actual life up to the standard of my ideals; I don't lower my ideals, although I can never hope to make them actual. It cannot be done by prayer or by education; it can only be done in the way Jesus Christ says, "Come to Me, all you who labor and are heavy laden, and I will give you rest." I will make the ideal and the actual one. The only way in which ideals can be made actual is by a personal relationship to God through Jesus Christ.

Solomon was the wisest and the wealthiest of kings, yet he says that "the plague of his own heart" knocked him out (see 1 Ki. 8:38). This is the first lesson every one of us has to learn. To begin with we are not prepared to accept Jesus Christ's diagnosis of the human heart, we prefer to trust our own ignorant innocence. Jesus Christ says, "Out of the heart of men proceed evil thoughts, adulteries, fornications, murders, thefts, covetousness, wickedness, deceit, licentiousness, an evil eye, blasphemy, pride, foolishness" (Mark 7:21-22).

No one has ever believed that. We have not the remotest conception that what Jesus says about the human heart is true until we come up against something further on in our lives. We are apt to be indignant and say—"I don't believe those things are in my heart," and we refuse the diagnosis of the only Master there is of the human heart. We need never know the plague of our own heart and the terrible possibilities in human life if we will hand ourselves over to Jesus Christ; but if we stand on our own right and wisdom at any second an eruption may occur in our personal lives, and we may discover to our unutterable horror that we can be murderers.

This is one of the most ghastly and humiliating and devastating truths in the whole of human experience. Our convictions are strong on the basis of innocence, and many a man out of havoc and sin and the changing of the gates of Paradise on the irreparable past, has to come to Jesus

Christ with a life exhausted by sin. Why should he? We know what Jesus Christ can do for an individual in that condition, but why cannot we see what He can do for the man who is not exhausted by sin? God does rescue the person who is down and out in sin, but there is no reason why any man should get there. Any man can get there, not one of us is immune. We may say—I don't know how he could do it. But we do. It is done by human beings just like you and just like me, without either our cowardice or our refinement. There is no virtue in not being bad on that line. It is because the vileness at the basis of the human heart has been closed over that we hear the talk nowadays of an "impossible chastity." Chastity is undesirable if I want to be a beast; but no holiness or rectitude of character is impossible; it is simply undesirable if I prefer the other way.

Education cannot deal with the plague of the heart, all our vows cannot touch it; the only Being who can deal with it is God through a personal relationship to Him, by receiving His Spirit after accepting the diagnosis of Jesus Christ.

Prospecting in Pursuit of Happiness
Ecclesiastes 7:25

"I applied my heart to know. To search and seek out wisdom and the reason of things, to know the wickedness of folly, even of foolishness and madness."

Solomon prospected to find out where the true essential enjoyment of life lay—was it in being an animal, an intellectualist, a governor, in being educated or uneducated? And he came to the conclusion that a man cannot find the true essential joy of his life anywhere but in his relationship to God.

Rationalism can never be the basis of things. Reason is my guide among things as they are, but reason cannot account for things being as they are. We do not think on the basis of Christianity at all. We are taught to think like pagans for six days a week and to reverse the order for one day; consequently, in critical moments we think as pagans and our religion is left in the limbo of the inarticulate. Our thinking is based not on Hebrew wisdom and confidence in God, but on the wisdom of the Greeks which is removed from practical life, and on that basis we persuade ourselves that if a man knows a thing is wrong he will not do it. That is not true. The plague with me, apart from the grace of God, is that I know what is right, but I'm hanged if I'll do it!

What I want to know is, can anyone tell me of a power that will alter my "want to"? Education will never alter the "want to," neither will high ideals nor vowing; that is where the great fundamental mistake in dealing with human problems has been made. It is only when a man is born from above of the Spirit of God that he finds the "want to" is altered. God does not take away the capacity to go wrong; if He did, we should not be worth anything. It is never impossible to go wrong.

We can only deal with the "sty" on the basis of redemption, not by thinking or by education, but only by redemption which is worked out by the Spirit of God.

Persecution and Peril
Ecclesiastes 7:26
"And I find more bitter than death the woman whose heart is snares and nets, whose hands are fetters. He who pleases God shall escape from her, but the sinner shall be taken by her."

The relationship of man and woman has been totally misrepresented. The revelation in the Bible is not that it is a question of the one being unequal to the other but of the two being one. "In the day that God created man, in the likeness of God made He him; male and female created He them and blessed them, and called their name Adam, in the day when they were created" (Gen. 5:1-2).[1] Man, the male being, took the government into his own hands and thereby introduced sin into the human race, and when God spoke He said that the Redeemer should come through the woman (see Gen. 3:15-16). The mother of Jesus Christ was a virgin. Redemption comes through woman, not through man.

Any young man who gets inveigled by the kind of woman Solomon is describing will find that the tendrils will remain to the day of his death unless God blasts them out by

---

[1] "In Adam and Eve we are dealing with the primal creations of God . . . . Eve stands for the soul side, the psychic side, of the human creation, all her sympathies and her affinities are with the other creations of God around. Adam stands for the spirit side, the kingly, Godward side. Adam and Eve together are the likeness of God, for God said: 'Let us make man in our own image, male and female, created He them.' The revelation made here is that woman stands not as inferior to man, but that she stands in quite a different relation to all things, and both are required to make the complete, rounded creation of God, referred to by the big general term Mankind. Eve, having this affinity and sympathy with the creation round about, would naturally listen with much more unsuspecting interest to the suggestion which came through the subtle creature that talked to her. The Bible says that Eve was deceived, the Bible does not say that Adam was deceived; consequently Adam is far more responsible than Eve, for Adam sinned deliberately. There was not the remotest conscious intention in Eve's heart of disobeying. She was deceived by the subtle wisdom of Satan via the Serpent. Adam, however, was not deceived in any shape or form; when Eve came to him he understood it was disobedience, and he sinned with a deliberate understanding of what he was doing, so the Bible associates sin with Adam (Rom. 5:12), and transgression with Eve (1 Tim. 2:14). (In this connection it is of importance to note that the Bible reveals that our Redeemer entered into the world by the woman) (*Biblical Psychology*, Ch. 3.)

redemption. The bands round his soul will never snap otherwise, it is impossible. The terror and iniquity Solomon is speaking of is being repeated over and over again in our day. The moral nemesis runs right through, and Solomon's counsel is right, the only way a man can escape is by pleasing God. If once these relationships are started in a man's life, the only thing he can do is to go to God, to scurry to Him like a rabbit. A man may give up the practices, but he will never escape the moral nemesis, it will haunt him in his unconscious personality. There is no power in vowing or education or forgetting that can release him, but "whoever pleases God shall escape," that is, committing himself to Jesus Christ and being delivered.

Solomon is not "slandering" woman, but pointing out that the result of sin in the human race is to have made the feminine part of Man which ought to be directly related to God, demoniacal if not so related. The one who hauls you nearer to God may be your mother or wife or sweetheart. If a woman's life is essentially related to God, her whole life is a sacrament for God; if not, her life may be a sacrament for the devil. The Bible reveals that the essentially feminine is meant to be the handmaid of God.

Any man or woman who falls in love comes right into God's presence, he or she instantly feels religious. Once love—my sovereign preference for another person—is awakened, it always goes direct to God like a homing pigeon. It is not hypocrisy on the part of a lad when he begins to pray, he cannot help it, his love is the finest lodestar in his life. That is the contrast between love and lust. Love can wait and worship endlessly; lust says—I must have it at once. The thing that can be hellishly wrong can be marvelously right.

Perfidiousness of Perpetual Relation of Man and Woman
Ecclesiastes 7:27-28

"Here is what I have found, says the Preacher, adding one thing to the other to find out the reason, which my soul still seeks but I cannot find: One man among a thousand I have found, but a woman among all these I have not found."

Solomon is not talking as a bitter disenchanted man. He is giving the Hebrew conception of things, that the counterpart of the woman is the man of God, and if she cannot find him she is either brokenhearted or she may become a woman of the devil. "I have looked for the essential wisdom in a man and have not found it; in a woman and have not found it there either." In human life as it is there is something perfidious in the perpetual relationship of man and woman.

Paul's counsel in dealing with marriage has been misrepresented—"Wives, submit to your own husbands," because we have taken the word "submit" to mean the obedience due from a slave to his master. It is not the obedience of an inferior to a superior, but the obedience of the equality of love. In the New Testament the word "obey" is used to express the relationship of equals. " . . . though He was a Son, yet He learned obedience by the things which He suffered."

"For the husband is head of the wife, as also Christ is head of the church." If Christ is the Head of the husband, he is easily the head of the wife, not by effort, but because of the nature of the essentially feminine. But if Jesus Christ is not the Head of the husband, the husband is not the head of the wife. Our Lord always touches the most sacred human relationships, and He says—You must be right with Me first before those relationships can be right; and if they hinder your getting right with Me, then you must hate them (see Luke 14:26).

Perfection and Perversion of Humanity
Ecclesiastes 7:29

"Truly, this only I have found; that God made man upright, but they have sought out many schemes."

The Bible states that God made man—the Federal Head of the race, in His own image. The only other Being in the image of God is Jesus Christ, the Last Adam. By eating of the fruit of the tree of knowledge of good and evil, Adam knew evil positively and good negatively. The Second Adam never ate of the fruit of the tree; He knew evil negatively by positively knowing good, and when a man is reborn of the Spirit of God he finds that that is the order God intended. Until we are born again we know good only by contrast with evil. The bias of the human heart is to find out the bad things first. How many of us are curious concerning the right way of life, concerning purity and nobility, and how many are curious to find out the borderland mysteries? The fruit of the tree of knowledge of good and evil has given human nature its bias of insatiable curiosity on the "sty" line. It is only after readjustment by Jesus Christ that the bias is on the other line, a tremendous thirst after God. "This is life eternal that they might know You."

Some Perspective
Ecclesiastes 8

". . . Life is not as idle ore,
But iron dug from central gloom,
And heated hot with burning fears,
And dipped in baths of hissing tears,
And batter'd by the shocks of doom
To shape and use."

—Tennyson

In the Diplomatic Service
Ecclesiastes 8:1-4

It is easy to despise the man above me because I know nothing about him, but Solomon counsels us to have a wider perspective, to look at things beyond our insular notions. It is a great education to try and put yourself into the circumstances of others before passing judgment on them. Solomon's counsel in these verses lies with those who in this order of things happen to be in the diplomatic service.

Courtiers' Discretion
"Who is like a wise man? And who knows the interpreta-

tion of a thing? A man's wisdom makes his face shine, and the sternness of his face is changed" (v. 1).

In Old Testament days if a man came before an eastern monarch with a sad countenance, he was liable to punishment (see Neh. 2:2). The discretion of a courtier does not make him a hypocrite, but puts him in the state of mind whereby his face indicates a strength and boldness which does not quaver. If you watch the faces of men who move much in diplomatic circles you will see exactly what Solomon indicates, an uninterpretable expression. The discretion of a courtier is to keep a bold face. Society is based on playacting; it must be. You cannot say what you really think; if you do, other people will, too, and if everyone were absolutely frank there would be no room for us!

The Bible point of view about government is that God compels man to govern man for Him, whether he likes it or not. The ordinance of government, whether it is bad or good government, does not lie with men, but is entirely in God's hands; the king or the government will have to answer to God (see 1 Pet. 2:13-14). The conservative attitude—My king, right or wrong—is a degeneration from the one great central point of the government of man by man.

God created a certain nation from the loins of one man, to be His own people; they were not to be like the other nations of the world, but to be the bond slaves of Jehovah until every nation came to know God (see Deut. 17:14-15). Israel and Judah said, "No, but we will have a king over us" (1 Sam. 8:19-20). The best kings Israel and Judah ever had were David and Solomon, and yet the most troublesome conditions as well as the most prosperous came during their reigns. Whether a king is of the order of the autocratic kings of the East, or the order of the Kaiser, the explanation of kingship, according to the Bible, is that it is the result of the wrong that entered into the world by the first man taking his rule over himself.

Hell is an eternal and an abiding distress to whatever goes into it. Whatever goes into hell can never again be established as a right thing. We say that militarism is going into hell just now; but militarism will crop up again in some form or another. *Something* has gone into hell, but it is difficult to say what.

Consistency to Decrees

"I counsel you, 'Keep the king's commandment for the sake of your oath to God' " (v. 2).

Anything bound before the king is bound as by the oath of God, and the consistency of a courtier is to abide by it. If a man lives in that order of things he must not be a traitor, he cannot take the action of a free individual man. The existence of peace and order depends entirely on this being remembered.

Character and Deportment

"Do not be hasty to go from his presence. Do not take your stand for an evil thing, for he does whatever pleases him" (v. 3).

Deportment is the way a man conducts himself. See that you neither hurry in nor out, says Solomon; your attitude must be both deliberate and careful. In the higher circles of social life this same thing is necessary.

It is an easy business for the man who deals in black and white to pass judgment on those who deal in gray. In the diplomatic service a man never deals with black and white, only with gray. For instance, it is easy to condemn British rule in India or in Egypt, but it is another matter to recognize the vast series of complications which the rulers in these countries have to face. In politics also it is difficult to steer a course; there is a complication of forces to be dealt with which most of us know nothing about. We have no affinity for this kind of thing, and it is easy to ignore the condition of the men who have to live there, and to pass condemnation on them.

Commands of Despotism
"Where the word of a king is, there is power; and who may say to him, 'What are you doing?' " (v. 4).

If a man is a courtier under a despotic king there is no possibility of replying; he has to obey to the last limit and has no right to a private opinion. The wise man is the one who knows when to speak and when to be silent.

In the Democratic Scrum
Ecclesiastes 8:6-10

All this has nothing to do with us, it is outside our perspective. How a king lives is a matter of moonlight to us; but one day we may have to pass judgment. Before long the democratic scrum may have to pass judgment on despotic kings, and before we can pass judgment we must have perspective. It is easy to condemn a state of things we know nothing about while we make excuses for the condition of things we ourselves live in.

The state of things resulting in the "democratic scrum," is better than the perfection of a machine. In our own country, rightly or wrongly, we committed regicide; France did the same. The world has never had to pay the price for either Britain or France that it has for Germany. Similarly, if

I never correct my child I am making a nice mess for other folks by and by. We have lost sight of these things, but they are elements we have to come in contact with.

Power to Wilfulness

"Because for every matter there is a time and judgment, though the misery of man increases greatly. For he does not know what will happen; so who can tell him when it will occur?" (vv. 6-7).

There is a power to wilfulness in man and when it is let loose there is the "wild ass" to account for; no matter what a man chooses, he heads towards evil.

Whenever a man is freed from a dominance that is ostensibly wrong, he has a power of will which may make for his misery. For example, this happened in connection with the freeing of the slaves; instead of using their freedom, many went back to their masters, while others abused their freedom.

Powerlessness of Willingness

"No one has power over the spirit to retain the spirit, and no one has power in the day of death. There is no discharge in that war, and wickedness will not deliver those who are given to it" (v. 8).

A man belonging to the democratic scrum may make up his mind that he is willingly going to do good, but no one can do it alone. The democratic rule is made up of people just like you and me, and unless we keep together, either by the right of a king or by the sway of some religious or civilized rule, we will kick things to bits, and the most willing among us will have the worst of it. "The divine right of kings" is a counterfeit for the true government of human life by man; at the same time it must be reckoned with.

We have to lay our account with the fact that the deepest bias in man is not toward God but away from Him, and if the man is allowed a right of way, he has a power of will which will increase the common misery. We have seen the hollow mockery of the diplomatic order of things under the divine right of kings, and today rightly or wrongly, we are all in the democratic scrum as never before; but neither autocracy nor democracy will solve the problem.

Price of Will Power

"All this I have seen, and applied my heart to every work that is done under the sun: There is a time in which one man rules over another to his own hurt" (v. 9).

The person who has power over another may hurt himself by the exercise of that power unless he himself is ruled by a greater power. If I have had a vivid religious experience and have power over people by means of that experience, the danger is that I usurp the place of God and say, "You must come my way; you must have this experience." This may damage you, but it damages me more, because my spirit is far removed from the spirit of Jesus Christ, it is the spirit of a spiritual prig. Whenever I exercise will power without at the same time being dominated myself, I damage something or someone.

Perversity of Will Worship

"Then I saw the wicked buried, who had come and gone from the place of holiness, and they were forgotten in the city where they had so done. This also is vanity" (v. 10).

Paul warns of the things which "have indeed a show of wisdom in will-worship," the idea that you are sufficient to govern yourself. We have got out of conceit with

Neitzsche's phrase, "the power to will"—if I have enough will I can do it.

The despotic rule is full of defect, misery and anguish, so is the democratic rule. Men may make all kinds of rules, but they get back again into despotism. Every man has power to go to hell because by nature his will is toward self-realization.

We may have no affinity with these things, but in passing judgment (and we never know when the time for passing judgment may come), we will be criminally unjust judges if we have not a true perspective. After the war it will not be a question of judging the autocrat but of judging the democrat, and the one is as bad as the other unless he is ruled by a power greater than himself.

In the Dispensational Scheme
Ecclesiastes 8:11-17

Patience of God and Bad
"Because the sentence against an evil work is not executed speedily, therefore the heart of the sons of men is fully set in them to do evil."

We say, Why does God allow these things? Why does He allow a despot to rule? In this dispensation it is the patient longsuffering of God that is being manifested. God allows men to say what they like and do what they like. (See 2 Pet. 3:14.) Peter says that God is longsuffering, and He is giving us ample opportunity to try whatever line we like both in individual and national life. If God were to end this dispensation now, the human race would have a right to say, You should have waited, there is a type of thing You never let us try.

God is leaving us to prove to the hilt that it cannot be done in any other way than Jesus Christ's way, or the human race would not be satisfied.

Patience of God and Good

"Though a sinner does evil a hundred times, and his days are prolonged, yet I surely know that it will be well with those who fear God, who fear before Him. But it will not be well with the wicked; nor will he prolong his days, which are as a shadow, because he does not fear before God" (vv. 12-13).

God allows the good to develop itself in the heart of the bad, and Solomon banks on the fact that the man who is rooted and grounded in confidence in God will come out right in the end. Nowadays we have the preaching of expediency: If you tell people that, they will take advantage of it. If the Almighty leaves His open knives around, it is not our business to put on the sheath. The rugged truths of God seem to give license to men; but do they? The prig notion makes us say certain things in order to terrorize people from doing wrong. But how much better are they if they don't do it?

The reward for doing right is not that I get an insurance ticket for heaven, but that I do the right because it is right. Honesty ceases to be the best policy if I am honest for a reason. "If any man will live godly, he shall suffer persecution." If a man wants success and a good time in the actual condition of things as they are, let him keep away from Jesus Christ, let him ignore His claims and the heroism of His holiness, there is no commercial value in it. In the final wind up it is the man who has stuck true to God and damned the consequences who will come out the best; whether he has made the best or the worst of himself in this life is another matter.

Preordination of God and Now

"There is a vanity which occurs on earth, that there are just men to whom it happens according to the work of the wicked; again, there are wicked men to whom it happens according to the work of the righteous. I said that this also is vanity. So I commended enjoyment, because a man has nothing better under the sun than to eat, drink, and be merry; for this will remain with him in his labor for the days of his life which God gives him under the sun" (vv. 14-15).

God's program for a man is *now*; not what he is going to do presently but what he is now. Solomon says your attitude to life as it actually is now, is to remember you are a man or woman, and that you have to live on the earth as a human being and not try to be an angel. It is your relationship to God which fits you to live on the earth in the right way, not necessarily the successful way. Sometimes you will have the worst of it for doing right.

Probation of God and Worry

"When I applied my heart to know wisdom and to see the business that is done on earth, even though one sees no sleep day or night" (v. 16).

Today men's hearts are failing them for fear. Our relationships involve a great deal more than "now," they involve the present and the children who are to come after them. How can they have faith in God when they see the security of the future hauled to bits? Solomon indicates that the wisest thing to do is to build our faith in God and not far-reach so that we have to watch everything and have no room for faith in God, no time to pay attention to how we live in the *now*.

Providence of God and Faith

"Then I saw all the work of God, that a man cannot find out the work that is done under the sun. For though a man labors to discover it, yet he will not find it; moreover, though a wise man attempts to know it, he will not be able to find it" (v. 17).

The summing up of the whole matter, says Solomon, is that you cannot locate yourself, you are placed in circumstances over which you have no control. You do not choose your own heredity or your own disposition, these things are beyond your control, and yet these are the things which influence you. You may rake the bottom of the universe, but you cannot explain things; they are wild, there is nothing rational about them. We cannot get to the bottom of things; we cannot get behind the before of birth or the after of death. Therefore the wise man is the one who trusts the wisdom of God, not his own wits. The amateur providence trusts his wits, and if he has not been knocked out by the hard problems of life, he can say cheap and nasty things; but when once he is hit by the real tragedy of life he will find it is not in the power of human wits to guide him, and he becomes either a man of faith or a fatalist.

Faith is trust in God whose ways you cannot trace, but whose character you know, and the man of faith hangs on to the fact that He is a God of honor. Fatalism means "my number's up," I have to bow to the power whether I like it or not; I do not know the character of the power, but it is greater than I am and I must submit. In this dispensation we do know the character of God, although we do not know why His providential will should be as it is. Solomon indicates that the only thing to do in the present condition of things is to remain true to God, and God will not only see us through but will see the whole thing out to a perfect explanation. That is the faith of a Christian, and it takes some sticking to.

Time, Death, and Trifles
Ecclesiastes 9

"If there be good in that I wrought,
    Thy hand compell'd it, Master, Thine.
Where I have fail'd to meet Thy thought
    I know, through Thee, the blame is mine.

Take not that vision from my ken;
    O, whatso'er may spoil or speed,
Help me to need no aid from men,
    That I may help such men as need!"

—Rudyard Kipling

We are apt to imagine that if we cannot state a thing in words it is of no value to us. What counts in talking and in reading is the atmosphere that is produced and what is opened up that would not be otherwise. There is a literature of knowledge and a literature of power. The former gives us informing stuff and we can say—This is what I have got. By the latter you cannot say what you have got but you are the better for it, your mind and heart are enlarged. We need more than information. The domain of things represented by the literature of power is that which comes with a knowledge of God's Book. One of the great secrets of life is that obedience is the key to spiritual life whereas curiosity is not only of no use but is a direct hindrance. When once a man learns that spiritual knowledge can only be gained by obedience, the emancipation of his nature is incalculable.

The Indiscernible Public Power of God
Ecclesiastes 9:1-2

"For I considered all this in my heart, so that I could declare it all: that the righteous and the wise and their works are in the hand of God. People know neither love nor hatred by anything that is before them. Everything occurs alike to all: One event happens to the righteous and the wicked; to the good, the clean, and the unclean; to him who sacrifices and him who does not sacrifice. As is the good, so is the sinner; and he who takes an oath as he who fears an oath."

Indiscernible—you cannot discern exactly why the power should take the turn it does. The old divines spoke of a miracle as "the public power of God." God emerges suddenly and does something beyond human power. Our Lord's miracles were cinema shows to His disciples of what His Father was always doing. (See John 2:1-11.) Our Lord never worked a miracle in order to show what He could do; He was not a wonder worker, and when people sought Him on that line, He did nothing. (See Luke 23:8-9.)

Solomon is referring to the indiscernible power of God in that He completely mystifies any calculations you may make in life. If you go on the mathematical or the rational line, you will come across something that can only be described as an act of God. You cannot say that because a man is good and has been well brought up and behaves well that he will reach success and prosperity; you will find that bad men who overreach and tyrannies come to prosperity while good men do not. (See Ps. 73:1-18.)

It is much easier not to look at the facts of life but to take an intellectual view which acts as a searchlight, and has the tyranny of an idea or an intuition. A man's intellectual view reveals what it does and no more, everything looks simple in the light of it; but when we come to the daylight of facts we shall find something that knocks the bottom board out of all our calculations. If you read a book by a philosopher about life, it looks as simple as can be, no complications or difficulties; but when you are flung out "into the soup," you find that your simple line of explanation won't work at all. Just when you thought you had found the secret, you find you are off the line.

Fundamentally, not shallowly, life can never be guided by principles. In the Christian domain we make the blunder of trying to guide our life by principles of Jesus Christ's teaching. The basis of Christianity is not primarily virtue and honesty and goodness, not even holiness, but a personal relationship to God in Jesus Christ which works out all the time by "spontaneous moral originality." Principles are of a lesser order, and if they are applied apart from the life of Jesus Christ they may become anti-Christian. Things cannot be worked out on a logical line, there is always something incalculable. You may think to reach your goal through obedience to a set of principles, but you will find it won't work that road. Solomon says that neither the good man nor the bad man ends where you expect him to. All you can say is that every man has his own setting from a starting point he knows nothing about. One of the finest and wisest books ever written for young men is *Leckie's Map of Life.* Leckie was not a genius, but a man of intense, moral earnestness and a careful intellectual collator as well.

The Interim Probationary Program of God
Ecclesiastes 9:3-4

"This is an evil in all that is done under the sun: that one thing happens to all. Truly the hearts of the sons of men are full of evil; madness is in their hearts while they live, and after that they go to the dead. But for him who is joined to all the living there is hope, for a living dog is better than a dead lion."

The Bible always states the obvious, and we find it to be the thing we have never looked at. Very few of us see the obvious, consequently when it is stated it strikes us as being original.

"For a living dog is better than a dead lion." "The Lord spoke to Joshua, saying, Moses My servant is dead"—now therefore go to mourning? No—"now therefore arise, go over this Jordan, you, and all this people, to the land which I give to them." The Bible never allows us to waste time over the departed. It does not mean that the fact of human grief is ignored, but the worship of reminiscence is never allowed. "We have to remember the departed and live in the light of them"—the Bible won't have it. "While the child was still alive, I fasted and wept; for I said, Who can tell whether God will be gracious to me, that the child may live? But now he is dead, why should I fast? Can I bring him back again?"

In the Garden of Gethsemane the disciples went to sleep when they should have watched with their Lord, and when Jesus came He said, "Are you still sleeping and resting? It is enough! Rise up, let us go." That opportunity is lost for ever, you cannot alter it, but arise and go to the next thing. We find this inevitable vanishing all through the Bible, and a man has to "ring out the grief that saps the mind." One of the most deeply ingrained forms of selfishness in human nature is that of misery. The isolation of misery is far more proud than any other form of conceit.

The interim between birth and death is a school training, a program of which we have not the laying out. We may calculate and say we are going to do this and that, but "you do not know what shall be on the morrow." It is a haphazard life, and we have to bank on God's wisdom, not on our own. It looks as if Solomon were counseling the Bohemian life, and as if Jesus Christ did the same when He said, "Therefore I say to you, take no thought for your life." A Bohemian is careless about everything, and neither Jesus Christ nor Solomon teaches that. Jesus Christ taught that a man is to be carefully careless about everything except his relationship to God. The great care of the life, Jesus says, is to make the relationship to God the one care. Most of us are careful about everything except that.

The life we are living has a program which we fulfill but about which we know nothing. We have been put into a program that we have no say in, and we bungle our part by trying to be our own organizers.

"There's a divinity that shapes our ends,
Rough-hew them how we will."

The Invincible Powerful Portion of Death
Ecclesiastes 9:5-6

"For the living know that they will die; but the dead know nothing, and they have no more reward, for the memory of them is forgotten. Also their love, their hatred, and their envy have now perished; nevermore will they have a share in anything done under the sun."

There is no further reward in practical existence for the

dead. We must lay our account with the invincible portion of death, it will come every time. Remember that your friend will die and act accordingly, and many a mean thing will wither on your tongue. There is a difference between sensitiveness and impressionableness. A sensitive man never says anything that would sting another, whereas the one we are apt to call sensitive is only impressionable to what stings him. Very few of us are sensitive; we are all impressionable. It is remembering the invincible portion of death that makes things different. Solomon says you cannot bank on insurance, or speculations, or on any kind of calculation. You can bank on only one thing, that your interim of life may at any second be cut short; therefore your only confidence is to remain true to God.

The Instructive Practical Prudence of Time
Ecclesiastes 9:7-9

"Go, eat your bread with joy, and drink your wine with a merry heart; for God has already accepted your works. Let your garments always be white, and let your head lack no oil. Live joyfully with the wife whom you love all the days of your vain life which He has given you under the sun, all your days of vanity; for that is your portion in life, and in the labor which you perform under the sun."

"Let your garments always be white"—live suitably attired to your station in life. Solomon's insistence is on the haphazard. These things—food, sex, money, and mother earth—must always have their place in the life of any man of God, and they either make men and women devils or make them what they should be. The man of God uses these things to express his relationship to God; whereas those who do not know God try to find lasting good in the things themselves. Paul, in riddling false religion, says that it will deny the basis of life, that is, it will teach abstinence from meats and marriage. The practical test of a man's life in time is how he lives in connection with these things.

The devastations of war are appalling, but there are compensations, and one compensation of this will be that we shall be driven back to the elemental. Some problems will not be revived again, they are finished; but every man will have a totally new attitude to these things and a new reverence for them. They will have a hold now which the refinement of civilization had made us lose.

The Imperative Performing Practice of Work
Ecclesiastes 9:10

"Whatever your hand finds to do, do it with your might; for there is no work or device or knowledge or wisdom in the grave where you are going."

The Bible nowhere teaches us to work for work's sake. That is one of the great bugbears of the anti-Christian movement in the heart of Christianity today. It is work with a capital W in which the worship of Jesus Christ is lost sight of. People will sacrifice themselves endlessly for *the work*. Perspiration is mistaken for inspiration. Our guidance with regard to work is to remember that its value is in what it does for us. It is difficult not to let ulterior considerations come in—"What's the good of doing this, we are only here for a short time, why should we do it as if it were to last forever?" Solomon's counsel is—"Whatever your hand finds to do, do it with your might" (RSV). He is not recommending work for work's sake, but because through the drudgery of work the man himself is developed. When you deify work, you apostatize from Jesus Christ.

In the private spiritual life of many a Christian it is work that has hindered concentration on God. When work is out of its real relation it becomes a means of evading concentration on God. Carlyle pointed out that weariness and sickness of modern life is shown in the restlessness of work. When a man is not well he is always doing things, an eternal fidget. Intense activity may be the sign of physical weariness. When a man is healthy his work is so much part of himself that you never know he is doing it; he does it with his might, and that makes no fuss. We lose by the way we do our work the very thing it is intended to bring us.

At the back of all this is the one thing God is after, what a man is, not what he does, and Solomon keeps that in view all the time. It is what we are in our relation to things that counts, not what we attain to in them. If you put attainment as the end you may reap a broken heart and find that all your outlay ends in disaster, death cuts it short, or disease, or ruin.

The Incalculable Precarious
Preference of Life
Ecclesiastes 9:11-12

"I returned and saw under the sun that—The race is not to the swift, nor the battle to the strong, nor bread to the wise, nor riches to men of understanding, nor favor to men of skill; but time and chance happen to them all. For man also does not know his time: Like fish taken in a cruel net, like birds caught in a snare, so the sons of men are snared in an evil time, when it falls suddenly upon them."

Life is immensely precarious, haphazard. A Christian does not believe that everything that happens is ordained by God; what he believes is that he has to get hold of God's order no matter what happens in the haphazard. "And we know that all things work together for good to those who love God, to those who are the called according to His purpose" (Rom. 8:28). All things are permitted by God, but all things are not appointed by God. They appoint themselves; but God's order abides, and if I maintain my relationship to Him He will make everything that happens work for my good. God on the one hand, myself on the other, and the rush of the haphazard in between will work toward the best.

"The race is not to the swift." The young man who is exceptionally clever at school very often becomes nothing afterwards; he attained too early. No one has any right to attain too early or mature too quickly. By the time he comes to the age of twenty or thirty the power that ought to mature is not there, he has ripened too soon. The boy who gives the grandest promise does not always become what you expect, while the one who is stodgy to begin with may come out on top. One of the finest commentators on the Bible was an ignorant dunce as a lad, with no promise at all to begin with.

There is always an incalculable element in everyone, therefore, Solomon argues, you cannot calculate. The crisis reveals what a man is made of. You cannot say what you would do in circumstances you have never been in because of this incalculable element, and when you are put in new circumstances you may suddenly find forces in yourself you never dreamed were there. You have no idea what is in you either for good or bad; you cannot estimate and say what you will do; therefore says Solomon, don't bank on calculations.

"For man also does not know his own time." You never know when your opportunity is going to come. Every man has to go out to sea to break from his moorings, whether by a storm or by a big lifting tide. There is a preference in life you cannot get at. Why does God choose one man and not another? "For exaltation comes neither from the east nor from the west nor from the south. But God is the Judge: He puts down one, and exalts another" (Ps. 75:6-7).

The Invidious Petulant Price for Wisdom
Ecclesiastes 9:13-16

"This wisdom I have also seen under the sun, and it seemed great to me: There was a little city with few men in it; and a great king came against it, besieged it, and built great snares around it. Now there was found in it a poor wise man, and he by his wisdom delivered the city. Yet no one remembered that same poor man. Then I said: 'Wisdom is better than strength. Nevertheless the poor man's wisdom is despised, and his words are not heard.' "

We do not put any price at all on wisdom when we have got what wisdom brings. When we attain success we do not remember the one who gave us the right counsel; the wise man who guided things aright is not taken into account. When a thing is done successfully in the army or the navy, it is very rarely the men of the regiment or the crew that are mentioned but only the figurehead at the top. Anyone with wisdom knows that that kind of preference is conceded, and there is no use losing heart over it. The discerning man understands that it is what lies behind the scenes that accounts for success.

In the same way there has often been a remarkably good but obscure woman behind a prominent man who has done great things. Solomon's counsel is to take into account the fact that you cannot expect to be recognized. Remember

that your lasting relationship is with God, otherwise you
will find heartbreak and disappointment and become cynical.

The Inveterate Popular Prejudice for Grab
Ecclesiastes 9:17-18

"Words of the wise, spoken quietly, should be heard
rather than the shout of a ruler of fools. Wisdom is better
than weapons of war; but one sinner destroys much good."

It is difficult to maintain a high standard when you are
working in a community which has a lower standard. For
example, we are told that the natives here do not understand any treatment but kicking and cursing and if they are
not treated in that way will take advantage of you. That
may be true, but you will also find that when they see you
are allowing yourself to be taken advantage of, they themselves will begin to climb. When we are over-reached most
of us get sick and give up. The counsel given by Jesus Christ
all through is on the line of abandon.

When a life is taken from the shelter of its ignorance it
goes through a state of transition, often worse than the stage
of ignorance, before it comes to real emancipation. Witness
the Reformation and the freeing of the slaves. In the transition stage we want to grab things for ourselves and ruin all
progress in life. Evolution, like Christian Science, is a hasty
conclusion. There may be nine facts which seem to make a
thing clear and conclusive, and one fact that contradicts.
There is always something that swerves away from the
explainable. The only explanation lies in a personal knowledge of God through Jesus Christ, not on the basis of philosophy or of thinking, but on the basis of a vital relationship
to Him which works in the actual condition of things as
they are. "I am the Way, the Truth, and Life."

Differentiations
Ecclesiastes 10

"Neither mourn if human creeds be lower
Than the heart's desire!
Thro' the gates that bar the distance
Comes a gleam of what is higher.
Wait till Death has flung them open,
When the man will make the Maker
Dark no more with human hatreds
In the glare of deathless fire!"

—Tennyson

It is one of the sharpest disillusionments to learn that "the best of men are but the best of men," and it takes us some time to learn that it is true. The apostle Paul brings out the same truth—Don't glory in men; don't think of them more highly than you ought to think. We always know what the other man should be, especially if he is a Christian. We are all lynx-eyed in seeing what other people ought to be. We erect terrific standards, and then criticize them for not reaching them. The standard of Christianity is not that of a man, but of God; and unless God can put His Spirit into a man, that standard can never be reached. According to New Testament wisdom and to Hebrew wisdom, until we are rightly related to God we will always be cruel to others. Take it in the matter of love: If I am not related to God first my love becomes cruel, because I demand infinite satisfaction from the one I love; I demand from a human being what he or she can never give. There is only one Being who can satisfy the last aching abyss of the human heart, and that is the Lord Jesus Christ.

The Best of Men Are But the Best of Men
Ecclesiastes 10:1-3

"Dead flies putrefy the perfumer's ointment, and cause it to give off a foul odor; so does a little folly to one respected for wisdom and honor. A wise man's heart is at his right hand, but a fool's heart at his left. Even when a fool walks along the way, he lacks wisdom, and he shows everyone that he is a fool."

How many remember that Solomon ruled Israel magnificently for many years? We remember his supreme acts of folly, and Solomon says that is the way human life is summed up. We remember the bad a man has done but not the good. It is possible to blast a man's reputation by raising your shoulders; but you can never blast his character. Character is what a man is; reputation is what other people think he is. "A long and splendid possible friendship has often been ruined by the agile cleverness of some men for labels." You meet a man and sum him up in a phrase. There were possibilities of his becoming a friend, but he will never be that now. This kind of clever business ruins the possibility of friendship.

Again we are apt to lose all distinction of right and wrong and to make excuses and say—Oh yes, there is always one fact more. "There is so much good in the worst of us and so much bad in the best of us, that it ill behooves any of us to talk about the rest of us." Although you know that the best of men are but the best of men, it is part of moral calibre to hold true to the highest you know, and to remember that "there is none good except one, even God."

"A wise man's heart is at his right hand; but a fool's heart at his left." A wise man's heart guides the decision of his mind; a fool makes a decision of mind and his heart drags after him.

In laying your account with men, whether it be with a government or with a drill sergeant, remember there is no such being as a perfect person. You are bound to find short-comings; and beware of the snare of remembering only the bad things someone does. We are all built that way.

The Besetters of Men and the Behavior of Men
Ecclesiastes 10:4-7

"If the spirit of the ruler rises against you, do not leave your post; for conciliation pacifies great offenses. There is an evil I have seen under the sun, as an error proceeding from the ruler; folly is set in great dignity, while the rich sit in a lowly place. I have seen servants on horses, while princes walk on the ground like servants."

Solomon is stating the obvious; most of us are too clever to be obvious. He is dealing with the man who happens to be placed under a providential order of tyranny. The diffi-culty of a man's behavior is the kind of men that beset him as rulers, and Solomon's counsel is amazingly shrewd: Let him say what he likes, it will blow over in time. In practical life it is the providential order of tyranny that embitters men more quickly than anything. We all shirk the counsel of Jesus Christ when he says, in effect, Never look for justice but never cease to give it. If you do look for justice, you will become bitter and cease to be a disciple of Jesus Christ. You are in a providential order of tyranny in which your behavior is to be determined by your previous relationship to God. That is, your conduct is to be determined by the relationship which reaches furthest back.

In the same way, if you are the servant of men for their sake you will soon be heartbroken; but if you serve them for the sake of Jesus Christ, nothing can ever discourage you (see 2 Cor. 4:5). Solomon's counsel is to keep your mouth shut if you are under a tyranny where you can gain nothing by expressing yourself. Behave yourself rightly, and if you wait long enough the thing will be put right. After all, the man who loses his temper quickest is the one who finds it quickest. The man you need to beware of is not the one who flares up, but the one who smoulders, who is vindictive and harbors vengeance.

"Folly is set in great dignity, while the rich sit in a lowly place." A ruler who is not wise places the fools in dignity through favoritism, and the man who lives at the basis of things and all in between have to be the cat's-paw of the man who has obtained his position through wire-pulling. You can never hold steady course unless you are rightly related to God first of all.

One of the most difficult things to do is to place men. Someone who knows men and can place them rightly is worth his weight in gold, and Solomon points out that such men are rare.

The "Before" of Men Determines the "After" of Men
Ecclesiastes 10:8-10

"He who digs a pit will fall into it, and whoever breaks through a wall will be bitten by a serpent. He who quarries stones may be hurt by them, and he who splits wood may be endangered by it. If the ax is dull, and one does not sharpen the edge, then he must use more strength; but wisdom brings success."

Many men are determinate, but not deliberate, and sooner or later they have to revise their decisions. The thing that comes after in a man's career is frequently determined by his having gone too hot-headedly into things to begin with. Don't be too earnest in clearing away the hedges. What makes me act determines the result of my action in the record of my life. Earnestness is not everything; I may be an earnest lunatic. We use the phrase "drunk and incapable," but it is just as possible to be sober and incapable. The great thing is to be enthusiastic and capable. Solomon's warning is that earnestness may often cover up an evasion of concentration in a life. John McNeill said about the student of Elisha who lost the axe-head—"If he had been of the modern school, Elisha would have said, 'Hit away with the stump, man; earnestness is everything.' "

Solomon points out that earnestness may be the characteristic of a fool. Earnestness in prayer is often put in the place of right relationship to God. If you read the New Testament carefully you do not find that Jesus Christ ever counsels earnestness in prayer, except in Luke 11, and there it is earnestness in connection with importunate prayer on behalf of others. The prayer Jesus Christ counsels is that based on simplicity. "But when you pray, do not use vain repetitions as the heathen do. For they think that they will be heard for their many words. Therefore do not be like them. For your Father knows the things you have need of before you ask Him." Prayer is never heard on the ground of earnestness, but only on the ground of redemption (see Heb. 10:19).

The "Beyond" of Men Decides
the "Breed" of Men
Ecclesiastes 10:11-15

"A serpent may bite when it is not charmed; the babbler is no different. The words of a wise man's mouth are gracious, but the lips of a fool shall swallow him up; the words of his mouth begin with foolishness, and the end of his talk is raving madness. A fool also multiplies words. No man knows what is to be; who can tell him what will be after him?"

If you are wise, you will lay your account with the fact that you cannot calculate. You cannot say that your charmer will charm the snake, it may sting you first. The before of a man's birth determines his breed. That one man is as good as another is a theory that does not work out in practice. Some are handicapped before they are born; others are perfectly fit before they are born, their heredity is clear. Breeding counts every time, but if you overbreed you produce genius and lunacy. Breeding counts for nothing in the value of a man in God's sight, it is the heart relationship that counts, and one man cannot judge another. When Jesus Christ came He paid no attention to breeding. In matters of practical living, says Solomon, if you are wise you will watch a man's breeding; but when you estimate men in God's sight, you must estimate from another standpoint, that of their relationship to Him.

The Beginnings of Mastery Disposes
the Mastered
Ecclesiastes 10:16-17

"Woe to you, O land, when the king is a child, and your princes feast in the morning! Blessed are you, O land, when your king is the son of nobles, and your princes feast at the proper time—for strength and not for drunkenness!"

When rulers eat in the morning they reorganize God's order and are simply shallow Epicureans. The man who masters men merely by his position determines the kind of men he masters. Some men are completely crushed and broken, sulky and taciturn, and their master is to blame. Whereas the influence of one man of integrity over men is incalculable; for example, Donald Hankey's *Beloved Captain*; and it is a terrible condemnation if a man's influence is without that characteristic. A man's character tells over his head all the time. The mastership of a man who does not defy the ordinances of God is that of worthship, he is worthy; whereas men who are mastered by those given to defying the law of God come to an appalling condition.

The Bungling of Men Spells the Beggary of Men
Ecclesiastes 10:18-20

"Because of much laziness the building decays, and through idleness of hands the house leaks. A feast is made for laughter, and wine makes merry; but money answers every thing. Do not curse the king, even in your thought; do not curse the rich, even in your bedroom; for a bird of the air may carry your voice, and a bird in flight may tell the matter."

"Because of much laziness the building decays." Solomon is pointing out that the bungling of men spells the beggary of men. "Whatever your hand finds to do, do it with your might." Our version of that too often is—"There's a thing to be done, but why should I do it?" Or, "Why should it be done properly, it is only for a little while?" That line spells beggary. No man if he is wise will be content with a knock-up job.

"Money answers every thing." Although money may cover up defects, yet ultimately it may lead to disaster.

"Do not curse the king, even in your thought." We cannot think anything without the thought having its consequence. Jesus Christ warns us of this—"With the same measure you use, it will be measured back to you." The basis of life is retribution, but our Lord allows no room for retaliation.

Timidities of Rationalism
Ecclesiastes 11

"Time was I shrank from what was right
From fear of what was wrong.
I would not brave the sacred fight
Because the foe was strong.

But now I cast that finer sense
And surer shame aside;
Such dread of sin was indolence,
Such aim at Heaven was Pride!"   —Newman

The boldness of rationalism is not in what it does, but in the way it criticizes. Rationalism is a method of criticism, but when it comes to action the rationalist is amazingly timid. Nothing bold has ever been done in the name of rationalism. In all the big crises of life the rationalist is at a discount. He is great at writing books, at pointing out the futilities of religion, etc., but no rationalist has ever produced the heroism, the adventure, or the nobility that the people and the things he criticized have produced. The reasonable man is, after all, the timid man, when it comes to certain things he refuses to venture.

We hear it said that Jesus Christ taught nothing contrary to common sense. Everything Jesus Christ taught was contrary to common sense. Not one thing in the Sermon on the Mount is common sense. The basis of Christianity is neither common sense nor rationalism, it springs from another center: a personal relationship to God in Christ Jesus in which everything is ventured on from a basis that is not seen. We are told that God expects us to use our "sanctified common sense"; but if we mean that that is Christianity, we will have to come to the conclusion that Jesus Christ was mad. If you go on the economical basis you get into confusion. Rationalism makes us timid, shrewd in criticizing, but nothing else. We never do the things that foolish people do.

The Counsels of Extravagance
Ecclesiastes 11:1

"Cast your bread upon the waters; for you will find it after many days."

Solomon states what our Lord elaborates in the Sermon on the Mount: that our reason for giving is not to be because men deserve it, but because Christ tells us to give. All through the Old and New Testaments the counsel is on the line of hospitality. As long as we have something to give, we must give. How does civilization argue? "Does this man deserve that I should give to him?" "If I give him money, I know what he will do with it." Jesus Christ says, "Give to him who asks you," not because he deserves it, but "because I tell you to." Some folks are so hyper-conscientious that they are good for nothing. Extravagance is the only line for the religious man. We do not believe this to begin with. We think we are so completely reasonable and sensible, consequently we base everything on self-realization instead of on Christ-realization.

The counsel of extravagance comes out all through the Bible. We are apt to ignore it by the timidity of our reasoning. The one thing Jesus Christ commended was Mary of Bethany's extravagant act. It was not her duty nor was it useful, and yet our Lord said that wherever His gospel should be preached "that what this woman has done will also be told as a memorial to her." The disciples, who were perfectly reasonable, said, What a waste! Jesus Christ said, "She has done a good work on Me." The true nature of devotion to Jesus Christ must be extravagance.

The Confusion of Economy
Ecclesiastes 11:2-4

"Give a serving to seven, and also to eight, for you do not know what evil will be on the earth. If the clouds are full of rain, they empty themselves upon the earth; and if a tree falls to the south or the north, in the place where the tree falls, there it shall lie. He who observes the wind will not sow, and he who regards the clouds will not reap."

Death transforms nothing. Every view of death outside the Bible view concludes that death is a great transformer. The Bible says that death is a confirmer. Instead of death being the introduction to a second chance, it is the confirmation of the first chance. In dealing with the Bible, bear in mind this point of view.

"Economy is doing without what you want just now in case a time may come when you will want what you don't want now." It is possible to be so economical that you venture nothing. We have deified economy, placed insurance and economy on the throne, consequently we will do nothing on the line of adventure or extravagance. To use the word "economy" in connection with God is to belittle and misunderstand Him. Where is the economy of God in His sunsets and sunrises, in the grass and flowers and trees? God has made a superabounding number of things that are of no use to anyone. How many of us bother our heads about the sunrises and sunsets? Yet they go on just the same. Lavish extravagance to an extraordinary degree is the characteristic of God, never economy. Grace is the over-flowing favor of God. Imagine a man who is in love with being economical! The characteristic of a man when he is awake is never that he is calculating and sensible.

Common sense is all very well in the shallow things, but it can never be made the basis of life, it is marked by timidities. We may say wise and subtle things, but if we bank on common sense and rationalism we shall be too timid to do anything. Today we are so afraid of poverty that we never dream of doing anything that might involve us in being poor. We are out of the running of the medieval monks who took on the vow of poverty. Many of us are poor, but none of us chooses to be. These men chose to be poor, they believed it was the only way they could perfect their own inner life. Our attitude is that if we are extravagant a rainy day will come for which we have not laid up. You cannot lay up for a rainy day and justify it in the light of Jesus Christ's teaching. We are not Christians at heart, we don't believe in the wisdom of God, but only in our own. We go in for insurance and economy and speculation, everything that makes us secure in our own wisdom.

The Confines of Exposition
Ecclesiastes 11:5-6

"As you do not know what is the way of the wind, or how the bones grow in the womb of her who is with child, so you do not know the works of God who makes all things. In the morning sow your seed, and in the evening do not withhold your hand; for you do not know which will prosper, either this or that, or whether both alike will be good."

The rationalist demands an explanation of everything. The reason I won't have anything to do with God is because I cannot define Him. If I can define God, I am greater than the God I define. If I can define love and life, I am greater than they are. Solomon indicates that there is a great deal we do not know and cannot define. We have to go on trust in a number of ways; therefore, he says, be careful that you are not too emphatic and dogmatic in your exposition of things.

A Christian is an avowed agnostic. I cannot find God out by my reason, therefore I have to accept the revelation given of Him by Jesus Christ. I do not know anything about God, things look as if He were not good, and yet the revelation given by Jesus Christ is that He is good, and I have to hang on to that revelation in spite of appearances.

"In the morning sow your seed," that is, don't bother about the origin of things. Solomon teaches all through the things that Jesus Christ insists on. Don't be careful whether men receive what you give in the right way or the wrong way, see to it that you don't withhold your hand. As long as you have something to give, give, let the consequences be what they may.

There is no possibility of saying a word in favor of a man after death if he did not do things before his death. The wisest thing is to make friends of the mammon of unrighteousness, that when you pass from this life they may receive you into everlasting habitations (see Luke 16:9).

The Consciousness of Experience
Ecclesiastes 11:7-8

"Truly the light is sweet, and it is pleasant for the eyes to behold the sun; but if a man lives many years and rejoices in them all, yet let him remember the days of darkness, for they will be many. All that is coming is vanity."

Solomon is stating the practical attitude to things in the midst of the haphazard. You have to live this actual life, he says, with your confidence based on God, and see that you keep your day full of the joy and light of life; enjoy things as they come. When we have a particularly good time, we are apt to say, "Oh well, it can't last long." We expect the worst. When we have one trouble, we expect more. The Bible counsels us to rejoice— "yet let him remember the days of darkness."

The Bible talks about drinking wine when we are glad (see Ps. 104:15); this is different from the modern view. It is bad to drink wine when you are in the dumps. Solomon is amazingly keen that a man should enjoy the pleasant things, remembering that that is why they are here. The universe is meant for enjoyment. "God, who gives us richly all things to enjoy." "Whatever you do, whether you eat or drink, do all to the glory of God." We argue on the rational line—Don't do this or that because it is wrong. Paul argues in this way: Don't do it, not because it is wrong, but because the man who follows you will stumble if he does it, therefore cut it out, never let him see you do it any more (see 1 Cor. 8:9-13). Solomon's attitude is a safe and sane one, that when a man is rightly related to God he has to see that he enjoys his own life and that others do too.

The Concentration After Expansion
Ecclesiastes 11:9-10

"Rejoice, O young man, in your youth, and let your heart cheer you in the days of your youth; walk in the ways of your heart, and in the sight of your eyes; but know that for all these God will bring you into judgment. Therefore remove sorrow from your heart, and put away evil from your flesh, for childhood and youth are vanity."

"For all these things God will bring you into judgment." "Judgment" means being brought into the arena of your own expansion. It is not that God is an almighty detective hiding round corners to catch and punish you, but that every time you have an expansion of heart or mind in your thinking you have to pay for it, and pay for it in an added concentration. There are times when we feel enlarged, we have met someone who has expanded our life; Solomon reminds us that we have to pay for that enlargement, and live up to the limit of the expansion by an added concentration. If we don't, we will come to a terrible smash. It is an appalling thing to see a young man with an old head on his shoulders; a young man ought not to be careful but to be full of cheer. "Rejoice, O young man, in your youth." Solomon is not advocating the sowing of wild oats, but that a man should enter into his life fully and remember that he must pay the price in the right way, not the wrong. When you have an opening up of your nature either in love or religion or adventure, you will have to pay for it in an added concentration. That means you have to bring all your life into keeping with the particular expansion; if you don't, you will become an arrant sentimentalist. To get hold of this truth is a big emancipation.

"Remove sorrow from your heart and put away evil

from your flesh." Youth is youth and age is age, and we have no business to require the head of age on the shoulders of youth. One of the affectations before the war was that we should never be enthusiastic about anything. That is not the style of a young man. According to Solomon, his life ought to be full to the last degree of expanding ecstasy, and he counsels him to do right things to the limit of his ability. Be enthusiastic and capable, go into things with all the vigor of life. But be prepared to pay for it. To pay for it means you must concentrate your life on a bigger plan; if you don't, you will become a dreamer. When a man has the vision of a poet or an artist, he has to learn to express himself, to become his own medium. There are more artistic people than artists because folks refuse to do this. Artistic people have art like a severe headache, they never work it out; they spurt out artistic ability, which is of no use to anyone. That is artistic disease, not art. Solomon's counsel is robust and strong—"Let your heart cheer you in the days of your youth; walk in the ways of your heart." The young man who cannot enjoy himself is no good, he has a sinister attitude to life. The man who can enjoy himself is not pretending to be what he is not. The best thing to do is to burn your bridges behind you, make things inevitable, and then go ahead.

The Dissolving Tabernacle
Ecclesiastes 12

We have been shown how to enjoy life. Now we are told of the days when such enjoyment abates. The sparkle of youth will depart. The keen sense of things is diminished; sun, moon, and stars are beclouded. This is a chapter of contrasts.

Lively Youth and Lingering Age
Ecclesiastes 12:1

"Remember now your Creator in the days of your youth."

We need a personal knowledge of God through all our life. The time to discover Him for ourselves is in Life's earliest morning—"And that from childhood you have known the Holy Scriptures, which are able to make you wise for salvation through faith which is in Christ Jesus" (2 Tim. 3:15). "And you, fathers, do not provoke your children to wrath, but bring them up in the training and admonition of the Lord" (Eph. 6:4).

We are so built that in childhood we can more easily come to a knowledge of God in simplicity than in later years. And in those formative years the personal life can be shaped and fitted to God's standard more surely than later on.

In the flower of your days when life is known in its rich fullness, when the natural powers are in undiluted vigor, then make place for God in personal consciousness. The prodigal remembered his father when he had spent all. He should have remembered him, gratefully, and with increasing understanding of his love and care, when his father was bestowing on him his goods. Love gives us all things richly to enjoy, and in youth and early manhood heaps rich precious bounties upon us. God must be remembered then, else we shall grievously hurt Him, and defraud ourselves.

"Before the difficult days come"—age with its infirmities is part of our human lot. Of Moses it was written, "His eyes were not dim nor was his natural vigor abated" (Deut. 34:7). But that was something unusual. There is "An Old Man's Parade" in the Bible, and we see decrepitude and frailty and fear showing their marks on bodily life. Isaac was old and his eyes were dim that he could not see. And Jacob too—"one told Joseph, Behold your father is sick," and the old man, sitting on the bed, stretched out his hands to his grandchildren. It is a pleasant sight to see the old man with his worn-out frame passing on the Divine blessing to those in their youth, and praying "The Angel who has redeemed me from all evil, bless the lads" (Gen. 48:16). We catch glimpses of the same thing in the New Testament: old Zechariah, and Simeon; there is "Paul the aged" and Peter ready to put off his earthly tabernacle. They had remembered their Creator in the days of their youth, and in their old age He was precious to them.

Luminous Skies aned Beclouded Vision
Ecclesiastes 12:2

"While the sun and the light, the moon and the stars, are not darkened, and the clouds do not return after the rain."

There is a loss of the sparkle of youth; there is not the same power of recovery after strain. How fascinatingly beautiful this earth can be to the keen vision of youth. The great poets wrote their abiding poems in their early years. It is God's order that the world should be a bright place for bairns. They have the capacity for entering into such natural joys; and it should not be denied them. There is a richer vision for mature minds who have been "born anew" and seen the Kingdom of God. Milton in his blindness saw rarer beauties than through the opened eyes of his youth.

Only the cynic will despise the loveliness and allurement of youthful days; but the saint will learn that even that bears the fatal hall-mark of "vanity." It too must pass. The happy delights of youth slip through our fingers as we hold them.

Lordly Mansion and Tumbling Dwelling
Ecclesiastes 12:3-5

"In the day when the keepers of the house tremble, and the strong men bow down; when the grinders cease because they are few, and those that look through the windows grow dim; when the doors are shut in the streets, and the sound of grinding is low; when one rises up at the sound of a bird, and all the daughters of music are brought low; also when they are afraid of height, and of terrors in the way; when the almond tree blossoms, the grasshopper is a burden, and desire fails. For people go to their eternal home, and the mourners go about the streets."

Man's body is frequently described under the figure of a house. What a lordly house his body is. We go back to watch its first construction in Genesis 1:27. The artistry of God is upon it all. Our bodies now are damaged by man's fall; but even so, how wonderful they are. No wonder we have the injunction, "Therefore glorify God in your body" (1 Cor. 6:20).

Verses 3-5 is a description of old age in its frailty. The keepers of the house (arms) and the strong men (legs) are weak and trembling; the grinders cease (teeth) and the windows are darkened (eyesight dimmed), the doors shut (ears are deaf), the grinding low (slow and tedious mastication), the easily startled nerves, and the loss of voice, the inability to climb, and the fear of highway traffic; the whitened hair like the almond tree in blossom, when any work seems a burden, and the failing natural desire, all portray the old man nearing the end of his earthly journey.

Life's Shapely Instruments and Death's Broken Things
Ecclesiastes 12:6

"Remember your Creator before the silver cord is loosed, or the golden bowl is broken, or the pitcher shattered at the fountain, or the wheel broken at the well."

The figures here used suggest the beauty and serviceableness of the human organs. The spinal cord as a silver chain, the shapely head as a golden bowl, the tireless heart as a household pitcher in constant use, and the circulatory blood system as a wheel in use at the well, all these show us life's vital ministry.

Until death invades and begins to destroy the precious things—the silver cord put out of action, the bowl broken, the pitcher broken, the wheel broken. Here is death in his fearsome aspect as house-breaker and destroyer. "The last enemy that will be destroyed is death" (1 Cor. 15:26). Our

Lord "became obedient to the point of death" (Phil. 2:8). "Knowing that Christ, having been raised from the dead, dies no more. Death no longer has dominion over Him"—nor us either (Rom. 6:9).

Languishing Dust and Ever-living Spirit
Ecclesiastes 12:7

"Then the dust will return to the earth as it was, and the spirit will return to God who gave it."

Man is dust and divinity. "And the Lord God formed man of the dust of the ground, and breathed into his nostrils the breath of life" (Gen. 2:7).

"Man is constituted to have affinity with everything on this earth. This is not his calamity, but his peculiar dignity. We do not further our spiritual life in spite of our bodies, but in, and by means of our bodies" (*Biblical Psychology*).

The dust shall return to the earth, but resurrection means the restoration of the full-orbed life of a man. What is sown a natural body will be raised a spiritual body. "This corruptible must put on incorruption, and this mortal must put on immortality" (1 Cor. 15:53).

The spirit that returns to God shall find future embodiment. Saints like Paul have had a deep longing to be clothed upon with "our house which is from heaven" (2 Cor. 5:1-4). Jesus Christ has brought to us His redemption which affects spirit, soul, and body. Already we experience an amazing spiritual renovation through identification with Jesus Christ in His death and resurrection (Rom. 6:4). But though we have received "the firstfruits of the Spirit," we are "waiting for the adoption, the redemption of our body" (Rom. 8:23).

Lessons of Truth and the Lodestar of Life
Ecclesiastes 12:9-14

"And moreover, because the Preacher was wise, he still taught the people knowledge; yes, he pondered and sought out and set in order many proverbs. The Preacher sought to find acceptable words, and what was written was upright—words of truth. The words of the wise are like goads, and the words of scholars are like well-driven nails, given by one shepherd. And further, my son, be admonished by these . . . Of making many books there is no end, and much study is wearisome to the flesh. Let us hear the conclusion of the whole matter. Fear God and keep His commandments, for this is the whole duty of man. For God will bring every work into judgment, including every secret thing, whether it is good or whether it is evil."

Wisdom expressed and analyzed must be received and applied for all it is worth. In the epilogue the instructor's scholarship concludes his frank and even devastating catalogue of human condition and behavior with its widespread complex of life's vicissitudes—its virtues and vices—its negatives and positives—its objectivity and subjectivity—when we might assume that he is agnostic and pessimistic but never atheistic—nevertheless, he shows us how not to live and thereby how we ought to live. He thrusts home with uncomfortable and poignant reality that which is vain and without value in this life "under the sun," that is, our earthbound, ground-level environment with its merely humanistic and even hedonistic perspective.

"The words of the wise are like goads." The goads of wise instruction serve to jab us out of our complacent acquiescence with our present evil world. Truths are spiritual realities that are fixed with an inexorable firmness and finality given and maintained by the one true shepherd Himself. They cannot be added to and must never be subtracted from. To be warned by the admonition, present in the Lesson of Truth, is to be made wise and balanced. We need not weary ourselves by wasting our time or energy on the unprofitable and unnecessary.

"Fear God and keep His commandments." Everything is summed up in verse 13. There is nothing more to say. The vital antidote to vanity with its apparent meaninglessness is this lodestar of life—reverence for God and obedience to His precepts and commands. The whole duty of man is to love Him with all the heart, mind, soul, and strength by being and doing what is according to His revealed will, recognized in His holy Word and based completely on the sure and solid ground of His perfect redemption.

In view of 2 Corinthians 5:10, that is, the final assize and the New Testament's full word on man's final form: "The earnest expectation of the creation eagerly waits for the revealing of the sons of God" (Rom. 8:19), faith will be consummated in sight "above the brightness of the sun" in His glorious presence. This is the end of the matter.

For that great hour we hope and long, when we shall pass from beneath the Shade of His Hand into the Full Shine of His Face.

Note to the Reader

The publisher invites you to share your response to the message of this book by writing Discovery House Publishers, Box 3566, Grand Rapids, MI 49501, USA. For information about other Discovery House books, music, or videos, contact us at the same address or call 1-800-653-8333. Find us on the Internet at http://www.dhp.org/ or send e-mail to books@dhp.org.

The Oswald Chambers Library

Spiritual guidance from the author of *My Utmost for His Highest.*
Powerful insights on topics of interest to every believer:

My Utmost for His Highest
Updated Edition—hardcover
Updated Edition—leather
Prayer Edition (Original)—hardcover
Large Print Edition (Original)—softcover
Audio Edition (Original)—12 cassettes

My Daily Journey With My Utmost for His Highest
by Carolyn Reeves
A companion to the golden book of Oswald Chambers.

Baffled to Fight Better
Job and the problem of suffering.

Biblical Psychology
Christ-centered solutions for daily problems.

Bringing Sons Into Glory &
Making All Things New
The glories of the great truths of salvation and redemption.

Christian Disciplines
Build strong Christian character through divine guidance,
suffering, peril, prayer, loneliness, and patience.

Daily Thoughts for Disciples
A collection of 365 daily readings from the best of a variety
of Chambers' writings.

The Highest Good &
The Shadow of an Agony—
Seeing life from God's perspective.

If You Will Ask
Reflections on the power of prayer.

The Love of God—
An intimate look at the Father-heart of God.

Not Knowing Where
A spiritual journey through the book of Genesis.

The Place of Help
God's provision for our daily needs.

Prayer: A Holy Occupation
A comprehensive collection of Chambers' writings on prayer.

Studies in the Sermon on the Mount
God's character and the believers conduct.

Shade of His Hand
Ecclesiastes and the purpose of life.

So Send I You &
Workmen of God
Recognizing and answering God's call to service.

About Oswald Chambers

Oswald Chambers: Abandoned to God by David McCasland
The life story of the author of *My Utmost for His Highest,* this volume unveils Chambers' active, devout, Christ-centered life from which flowed this century's best-loved devotional book.

Order from your favorite bookstore or from:

Discovery House Publishers
Box 3566
Grand Rapids, MI 49501

Call toll-free: 1-800-653-8333